Retail Analytics

Wiley & SAS Business Series

The Wiley and SAS Business Series presents books that help senior-level managers with their critical management decisions.

Titles in the Wiley and SAS Business Series include:

For more information and a complete list of books in this series, please visit www.wiley.com/go/sas.

Retail Analytics

The Secret Weapon

Emmett Cox

WILEY

John Wiley & Sons, Inc.

Published by John Wiley & Sons, Inc., Hoboken, New Jersey.
Published simultaneously in Canada.

For general information on our other products and services or for technical support, please contact our Customer Care Department within the United States at (800) 762-2974, outside the United States at (317) 572-3993 or fax (317) 572-4002.

Wiley also publishes its books in a variety of electronic formats. Some content that appears in print may not be available in electronic books. For more information about Wiley products, visit our web site at www.wiley.com.

Library of Congress Cataloging-in-Publication Data:

Cox, Emmett.
   Retail analytics : the secret weapon / Emmett Cox.
      p. cm.—(Wiley & SAS business series)
   Includes index.
   Summary: "Retailers have collected a huge amount of data but they do not know what to do with it. This book is designed not only to provide a broad understanding of retail but show how to use the data that these companies have. Each chapter covers a different focus of the retail environment from retail basics and organization structures to common retail database designs. Numerous cases studies and examples are given throughout. In addition, within each chapter the importance of analytics and data is examined"—Provided by publisher.
   ISBN 978-1-118-09984-1 (hardback); ISBN 978-1-118-14835-8 (ebk);
   ISBN 978-1-118-14832-7; ISBN 978-1-118-14834-1 (ebk)
   1. Retail trade. 2. Retail trade–Statistics. 3. Retail trade–Case studies. I. Title.
   HF5429.C683 2012
   658.8'7–dc23

                                                                              2011023738

Printed in the United States of America

10 9 8 7 6 5 4 3 2

Contents

Preface

Through my years in analytics, and particularly in retailing, I have had the great opportunity (and, to some extent, struggle) to work with analysts and businesses from many different countries. As analysts, we try to see problems in black and white, with as little gray area as possible. What may be seen as obvious in one country, however, is a new concept in another. Managing many different analytics teams and projects across these countries became somewhat of a learning and teaching exercise. I was (and happily still am) constantly learning about the different cultural nuances of each country. One such difference comes from the use of prebuilt software. One of my teams was up on all the latest software and felt that this gave them a competitive advantage in developing quick and effective analytic solutions. One specific team in another country felt that many software solutions were nothing more than black boxes, secret systems that could not be replicated, and that they would rather write the code themselves and develop the modeling required so that each solution would be tailored to the client's needs.

While these differences can be overcome, the majority of my time dealing with global teams was spent explaining what type of analysis I need to get completed. This may sound simple, but when the basic retail terminology was missing, the management task became enormous. With so many young and intelligent MBAs with little first-hand experience in retailing, how do you explain stock-keeping units or package quantities, much less market basket analysis with trade area overlays?

With every country in a different time zone, it was difficult to have everyone on a call at the same time to explain some of the basic retail analytics fundamentals. So, I began my four-year attempt to write down all of the retail analytics information that I had gathered from my 30-year retail career. At the time, I was just hoping to get my teams on an even level with one another with basic terms and concepts, which was totally self-serving, as I wanted to cut back on my 2 A.M. and 3 A.M. conference calls. What I finally ended up with is a book filled with examples of projects and solutions, along with a complete list of terminology that I have used across my broad retail background. I had no idea that this would end up in a book, much less be sought after by acquaintances across the world. I am humbled by this, because this book was a labor of love.

This book is intended to be a reference guide, which should help in developing a better understanding of retailers' language and analytic process. I have included a glossary of terms that are commonly used by retailers as well as a list of retail-oriented projects. No project can be a failure if you learn from the outcome. Try to be creative in your pursuits to solve business hurdles. Your creativity can be your best asset. Analytics is an art as much as a science and you need to keep balance.

I have included examples of projects and case studies that I have either developed or brought to fruition based on someone else's request.

I have a deep retail and financial services background, and blend both perspectives in my writing. I also at times strive to keep the credit-card marketing point of view in scope. A predominant theme throughout this book is "This credit stuff is okay, but what does it do for my merchandise sales?" This is a common theme for retailers at all levels. Keep this in mind as you read through each section.

As each project is thought out, discussed, and presented, there has to be either some measurable positive impact to the client's business, an increase in credit card usage (increased share), or some dramatic increase in the client relationship position (would the retailer recommend you to his peers?). Ideally, we would like to influence all of these factors.

For the best results, refer to the glossary of terms at the end of the book. Understanding these terms will help your ability to use each concept.

Acknowledgments

While this book was a labor of love on my part, it took many people over the years to help me gather the inquisitive analytics spirit to try so many differing retail avenues. I must thank Kmart Corporation as a whole for placing me on the leadership fast track, which meant moving me to a new division every two to three years. I never had a chance to get bored. Over a 27-year career that encompasses many different areas, I began my career pushing buggies and ended up 23 years later managing the complete database marketing for the company. This hands-on experience has been invaluable throughout my career.

I need to single out Tom Lemke, whom I met when he was the vice president of marketing for Kmart. I have had the opportunity to continue working with Tom over the years. Tom has a great mind for seeing the future, and has always pushed me to either prove or disprove his concepts with hard-core analytics. This constant challenge has pushed me to continually try new methods and concepts to validate strategic and business processes.

I wish to thank David Fogarty, the vice president of Global Decision Sciences for GE Money, for his belief that global retail analytics has a place in a large organization. His constant support was very much appreciated.

I also thank Skander Malcolm, the CEO of GE Money for Australia and New Zealand, for his belief that retail analytics could drive sales and profitability for our partners and GE alike. His constant and unwavering belief that I could make a difference in my overseas assignment gave me the confidence I needed. I still follow his advice.

Tom Davenport, although a great author himself, always takes the time to speak with aspiring authors and offer advice. Tom has spent more than his fair share of time convincing me that I should complete this project and set a deadline. I followed his advice, which is one reason this book was finally completed. Tom, thank you for being a great inspiration.

I have to thank my wife, who has had the patience to put up with my frequent trips out of the country and late nights working with my global teams. She has always been a great partner in these efforts. She is always there to remind me that "every great man has a woman telling him what to do." Who am I to argue this point? She is my best friend and has been for 30 years.

Over my career I have met so many individuals that have helped frame my diverse perspective on business and analytics that I cannot possibly name them all. All I can say is thank you, and hope that I continue to meet more of you.

CHAPTER 1

Retailing Analytics: An Introduction

T he purpose of this chapter is to help develop a basic understanding of retail terminology and concepts across a wide variety of backgrounds and experience levels. The one constant factor is that we are all using analytics in some form in the support of our organizations.

A significant portion of my work over the past seven years has involved using data from consumer credit card programs to improve retail in many areas. Credit card data can be found in various levels of detail, from bin range at the transaction to aggregated card type (Visa, MasterCard, etc.). I include the use of credit data within the various sections and show how it was used to improve many types of analytics.

I also include perspectives from the credit card companies, as many of these companies do not have any practical retailer experience. They constantly struggle trying to find a bridge between credit and retail. I have found analytics to be a great bridge between retail and credit companies, as the data provided by both, when combined, can be an extremely important source of insights. Helping these credit companies understand retail organizations will, in the end, help retailers.

RETAILER GOODWILL

Goodwill can be described as those warm and fuzzy feelings that make the clients feel that you have their best interests at heart, and it is important to show that you and your analytics team are not singularly focused on your business at the expense of the retailer's business. Fuzzy metrics are very hard to measure mathematically and, as such, are difficult to grade for performance. Customer relationship management (CRM) is all about the customer, which, in this case, is your client, the retailer. While in the global General Electric (GE) role, GE analytics teams had to manage the customer-client relationship. But instead of just getting the end customer to use more of our card services, we also wanted to have a positive influence so that the clients (retailers, in most cases) would request more products from GE, seek more consultation from analytics, and allow us more involvement within their inner circle. All of these outcomes are very positive, but again, difficult to equate back to any financial gain. Do not lose sight of the importance of these soft benefits; they can be long-term relationship builders. One aspect that can be measured is contract continuation versus renegotiations. Another strong indicator of how the client is feeling toward you is its willingness to recommend either you or your organization to its peers, often referred to as a net promoter score. This can be absolutely invaluable in the business community, and is now a key performance indicator (KPI) in evaluating many businesses.

THE INSIDE SCOOP: RETAIL POWER BROKERS

More often than not, the merchants and buyers are the real operators within the retail business. They pay the bills and bring in the profit. If you can show that increased credit card usage or fact-based analytics will sell more products, they will listen. Remember, the retailer business is selling merchandise, not credit.

Also keep in mind that these are increasingly competitive times for all retailers, and saving fees can be a very important aspect of the retailer's budgeting. So, interchange fees (those fees paid to process credit card transactions) can be of interest to finance and the budgeting areas, but of little interest to the merchants. If you can show that data usage will give the buyer (brand manager) a competitive advantage, she will pay attention.

Almost without fail, retailers are set up in a hierarchical arrangement. There will be different groups within the merchant buying area, usually apparel, hard lines, commodities, sporting goods, and so on. While managing the credit card analytics area, I have found it easiest to align with the head of one merchandise area that best suits credit card marketing, maybe an early adopter (someone who easily accepts new concepts). When you align with this person, try to make it a win for the retailer with some tangible benefits for the card. Once you have some incremental cases that show a win for your partner, you are now able to begin some peer pressure tactics—"If this worked well for partner X, why don't you try this, too?"

This process takes patience and time, but it is well worth the effort. Remember, the merchants are without doubt the *moneymakers* for retailers, and hold the influence. Having them as partners is important and worth the effort. It is crucial to understand the retailers' language, and to communicate back to them in terms they understand and feel comfortable with. If you are to gain their trust, they have to be comfortable that you understand them and their business.

RETAIL ORGANIZATION

Within most retailers, there is a basic organizational structure. The unit that brings in the profit is the merchandise group, most often managed by the general manager or vice president. This individual will be in charge of a full line of merchandise (e.g., apparel, commodities, groceries, entertainment). Below this level is the lead buyer, who would manage a line of goods (e.g., produce, women's slacks, or electronics). A vice president may have as many as five lead buyers, depending on the range of products the retailer carries. Next would be a co-buyer who manages the item-level products within a single category. Another buyer that plays an important role is the re-buyer, who, in most cases, is located at the distribution center (DC). This buyer maintains the ordering flow of the goods into and out of the DC.

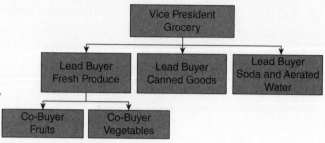

Exhibit 1.1 Organization Chart

Understanding how retail businesses are organized is an important and necessary step. Many follow the standard design as shown in Exhibit 1.1. This design shows a clearly defined break in the hierarchy. Each level of the organization will require different levels of analytics support and reporting (summary versus detail). This is a simple view of a retail merchant chart.

A standard organization chart would look like this:

- One vice president: grocery
- Four or five lead buyers: produce, canned goods, aerated waters, and so on
- Four or five co-buyers: fruits, vegetables, and so on

Having the buy-in to your project at each level is ideal, but not always possible. Knowing the buying organization for your particular industry or retailer is critical. Each area can be particularly territorial, and being able to associate your idea with their level of control is very important.

Many organizations are developing executive information systems (EISs) for the more senior members of the organization. These are more interactive approaches to information retrieval. These systems use special reports called dashboards and are supported by smaller subsets of the organization's databases, called cubes. Cubes are fairly complex, but for the purposes of this discussion, consider them to be big servers with predefined fields that allow for the quick loading and retrieval of specific information. Because the information fields on the cube are fixed, the fields do not change, only the most recent information does. For example, the sales data from Division One is available, so you can view this information. The most recent sales information for the division level is always loaded and kept current. If you wanted to see the department-level sales, however, you would have to make a special request, as this was not designed in up front. This sounds complicated, but it is very common.

As you move down from the senior executives, you generally find less automation in the reporting and more complexity in the level of analytics. The senior group would want to know how sales are compared to the previous year. The next level down would want to know which regions were above or below the previous year. As you move down, the questions become much more exact in their analytics requirements. I have found that the questions from the senior group are more strategic and are big questions requiring more time to organize. The questions at the manager level seem to be more tactical in nature: There are far more questions and they are far more detailed.

Another observation about retailers that they use the term *marketing* liberally. There are all sorts of marketing roles across a retailer; I touch on just a few.

Real Estate Marketing

In real estate marketing, you will try to identify where new stores should be built. This starts off with field representatives looking at an available property and determining whether it would be a good location. There is a whole team of analysts working on an evaluation of the sales potential, the existing competitor influence, and the logistics of getting the merchandise to the store, not to mention where the new consumers are and how they would get to the store. You then bring in the finance support team, which again can be part of the real-estate marketing department. Their role is determining what breakeven would be, and how long the store would have to be open to achieve this magic number. I worked in real estate marketing for a few years and found it fascinating and a great learning experience. The range of high-level SAS analytics was extensive, from designing distance and square-foot algorithms to building models to determine the transfer rate of sales from specific competitors. Transfer rates are the effect of moving sales from a consumer at Store 12345 to Store 45678. This sounds simple, but it is really very complex. GIS, or geographic information systems (detailed in Chapter 4), are an integral part of this department, as the utilities for calculating multiple factors at the same time are enormous. If you like high-powered analytics and learning about vector and thematic mapping, I would highly recommend this field.

Creative Advertising Marketing

Creative advertising is more of a traditional marketing area, in which you work with the design side of the business. Which colors are in trend right now, what products should be advertised to bring in more shoppers, and what type of media should be used (e.g., radio, television, print, or billboard)? This area can also include which geographies to advertise in, which could be the local television network or a cable network. Many times, this area has an analytics team to help develop the results of each promotion, and can include very advanced market-mix analysis. There are times—quite frequently, actually—when multiple media are running at the same time. To judge which media type was contributing the most to a product's sale, a technique called media-mix modeling is used. This technique weighs each of the particular media and assigns some portion of the promotional sales back to it. This is very oversimplified, but that is the basic premise.

Operations Marketing (Research)

Operations marketing falls within the marketing organization, even though operations typically resides in the research function. This includes developing many qualitative consumer studies (focus groups, exit surveys, store intercepts, and so on). Each of these studies consists of asking a set number of consumers a list of questions from which you can tabulate the answers and form a qualitative opinion. There is a science to developing the correct group of questions surrounding a particular business need, and asking the question under the correct context is critical. Focus groups are composed of a group of preselected individuals that fit a certain makeup (that is, they have shopped your store, have used your credit card, or have purchased your brand in the last 60 days). The group is brought into a room and asked general, preselected questions by a moderator who keeps the discussions moving toward some logical conclusion.

Exit surveys involve stopping consumers as they leave your store, a mall, or some other location where a lot of people congregate (typically malls). Again, they are asked specific questions, but generally no more than seven or eight, as the more time you take from the shopper, the less relevant the answers will be.

Store intercepts involve stopping consumers while they are still shopping to ask them very pointed questions. Why did you pick up product X today, or why did you walk by product Y today?

Many times consumers are stopped as they enter a store and are asked a number of questions about their current trip. These same consumers are then intercepted on their way out of the store and their receipts are logged against what they said they intended to buy. These studies are very rigorous, but can be extremely informative, as consumers do not always do what they say they are going to do.

Direct Marketing

Next is direct marketing, which is sending mail out that is directly addressed to a particular individual at a specific address. This area is aligned very closely with the CRM and database management group, as direct marketing depends heavily on clean, accurate, consumer-rich data. The biggest concern of direct marketing is to have the correct name and address for the individual being targeted. Next is to be sure you are offering something relevant to the individual (for example, sending a coupon for $1.00 off dog food does not make a big hit if the household does not have a dog).

Strategic Marketing

Strategic marketing is a compilation of most of these previous areas. The big effort here is to plan out the next five years of the business's marketing efforts. Whom do you want to market to? Who will your target consumer be in the next five years? What types of messaging will you use to reach this consumer? How will you gain market share? To fully understand these types of questions, the strategic marketer needs extensive store-level experience along with operations, marketing, and many other forms of background. This area is not for the weak-hearted individual, as team members are often called upon by senior leadership to lay out the company's plan from many different perspectives, on very short notice.

There are a few more, but this covers a great majority of the different types of marketing within a typical retail business.

COMMUNICATING TO THE RETAIL ORGANIZATION

Knowing the correct terminology is a key area; if you do not know the proper terms for the industry, you must do some research. In retail, these terms are used in everyday discussions, and are the minimum level of knowledge:

- *Case pack:* Products are shipped in full cases (for example, 12, 24, or 36 units). These types of products cannot be broken down into smaller quantities.

- *Divisions → Departments → Categories → Subcategories → Baselines → Color → Size:* These are all part of the merchandise hierarchy.

- *Drop shipping:* Prepacking merchandise so that a pallet or large case can be dropped at a store without sorting.

- *EAN:* European article number. This is a European version of the UPC (described below).

- *General merchandise:* Nonfood types of merchandise.

- *Gross margin:* The difference between cost and selling price (revenue minus cost of goods sold).

- *JIT:* Just-in-time shipment.

- *Logistics:* The routes many trucks take to deliver goods from a central warehouse to a store.

- *Markdown:* How much a product will be reduced in price from the listed price.

- *Mark-on:* A term interchangeable with *markup*, indicating the profitability of a product.
- *Pack quantities:* Package quantities designate how many items will be packed in a single bundle.
- *POS:* Point of sale cash registers.
- *Price type:* Regular, markdown, event, rain check, BOGO (buy one, get one free), or clearance.
- *Season code:* A number designating the seasonal nature of a product.
- *SKU:* Stock-keeping unit. This is the basic term for a piece of merchandise.
- *UCC:* Universal Code Council. This council sets the standards for all UPCs.
- *UPC:* Universal product code. This is a bar code that is assigned to a single piece of merchandise.

These are very common terms that are easily understood within the retailers' walls. The more you can fit these terms into your strategy or discussion, the better their impression of you will be. Remember to refer to the back of this book for a full glossary of terms.

POINT OF SALE VERSUS MARKET BASKET DATA

Point of sale data is stored at the SKU (that is, single-product) level. For example, 1,000 pieces of SKU 12345 were sold last week; 12,000 widgets were sold today.

Market basket data includes the relationships between all items within the associated basket together. This ties the purchase history together, which, in turn, builds item affinities (the relationships between those products most frequently purchased together).

Advanced market basket data also includes a customer identification number. With this, you can track purchases over time. Without the time series (over time by day, week, and season) of the data, the value of the data goes down considerably. Tracking changes in purchase behavior over time allows for much stronger variance models, as well as predictors.

You need to be aware of the types and breadth of data that your retailer will have access to (both internal and external data). When beginning to evaluate the retailer's data sources, if appropriate, ask if he will share some of the data with you (demonstrate that there is an incremental benefit). Retailers will most certainly have much more data available to them than they can absorb. The most difficult hurdle to overcome is gaining their trust. One tactic I have used in the past was to offer to evaluate an issue unrelated to credit data for the retailer. We were able to use our advanced analytics approach to provide the retailer with a different perspective on a problem he was facing. This single project opened the doors to more data, which allowed us to provide a better product to both the client and the cardholders.

It also helps if you can be aware of the external data sources that your retailer is using in her business. Sources such as Spectra Marketing, ACNielsen, Claritas, NPD group, and Trade Dimensions, to name a few, can be a tremendous boost to any analysis. By being familiar with retailers' data sources, you can better understand their analytics capabilities. If the retailer will not share this information with you, it is easy enough to determine it on your own through Internet searching.

It is also helpful if you can identify what your retailer's best competitor is using as far as additional data sources. Depending on what level of data they are buying and the breadth of companies they are buying it from, you can get a good insight into where they are headed strategically.

DATA IS GOLD

All merchandise has a life cycle: from the day a store opens for the first time, when the opening inventory is estimated (based on historical data), through the sales of the product, which triggers an order for more. This sale creates a ripple effect that can be felt around the world. If a chair is sold, the register sends a data file to the inventory system for that supply chain, indicating that a chair was sold and the supplier should send another one. If there is one in the DC, it is sent to the store as replenishment.

Now the DC needs to replenish its own stock to be prepared for the next sale. The DC will send a request for merchandise to its supplier (the vendor). These suppliers tend to not keep merchandise in stock, but take orders for future shipments, which are sent out to the raw materials' manufacturers. Many of these manufacturers are now located in places such as China, Taiwan, and Hungary, which may be a considerable distance from your store.

To build a chair, the manufacturer in China buys raw materials from many local areas. The chair is then sent to a re-buyer who works for a supplier that maintains the movement of products to the vendor that keeps shipping the product to the retailer.

This process all started with a single piece of data that was triggered at the POS register.

The next time you buy a newspaper or a chair at the retailer in your neighborhood, think about the process you just triggered.

This is a very simplistic view of a very complex and difficult process. I could go on in great detail about the different types of replenishment, such as JIT, but there are many books on the subject by experts that specialize in just that.

When I started out in retail, we used list books and area merchandisers who would walk down each aisle, writing down how many products of a particular SKU were on the shelf. Each merchandiser had his own department to keep track of, and this process was begun on Monday and continued all week. The list book also noted the case pack (that is, how many units were in a single order) so that we would know when to place the order. Once counting on the sales floor was completed, we would go to the stockroom to count the merchandise back there. We had to calculate the rate of sale (that is, three per day, five per week, and so on) to judge how many products we needed to order so that we did not run out. We kept track of how long it took to get the merchandise to our store so that we did not run out of anything. If we had six on the counter and zero in the stockroom, with a rate of sale of two per day and a ship time of three days, we needed to order right away.

We progressed to trigger figures, using a number—again, written in the list book—that told us the optimal quantity of units to have on hand before we placed an order. This was considered very advanced back then, as we could have more people do the ordering without the need for special training. All of these changes were precursors to the modern POS replenishment systems of today. These are obviously much more advanced, but still work from the same principles.

DATA AS REVENUE: THE PRICE OF RETAIL DATA

There are many companies that buy and sell retail sales data. Some of this data is at the POS SKU level (a single product view), while a smaller number of retailers also sell data at the much lower market basket level (with all product associated back to a single transaction). Depending on the size and scale of data and the quantity and breadth of time span, the retailers can make significant amounts of revenue. This figure can be as much as $20 million to $30 million on an annual basis. There are a few big-name companies, such as ACNielsen, NPD, and IRI, that aggregate retailer data at some point. These third-party firms consolidate the data from many different retailers in such a way as to hide the identity of any one company. They then package it and sell it to both retailers and manufacturers. This data gives an industry perspective and is a very valuable piece of the category management philosophy.

Many manufacturers buy nonaggregated data to help identify what products from other companies are competing directly with theirs, from a retailer perspective. These data points are gathered by collecting purchases at the household level. ACNielsen, NPD, and others have households that collect purchase data through the use of scanners. As the products are brought home, each UPC is scanned and entered into a diary that is transmitted back to the parent company. The company collects information on where the products were purchased, the date and time of purchase, the selling price, and the product specifics. These companies have as many as 150,000 households across the United States participating in these surveys.

To really make this data valuable to both retailers and manufacturers alike, these companies need to add in retailer POS data. These companies will pay quite a bit, depending on the breadth of merchandise categories and the sales volume (that is, number of stores and number of transactions). At one of my retailers, we were able to develop a self-sustaining marketing analytics department by selling specific categories of merchandise data to just one data company.

In Chapter 2, "Retail and Data Analytics," I cover some technical data storage suggestions in much more detail and go into depth on specific analytics case studies. These case studies cover a broad range of topics and include e-business and online cross-channel techniques.

CHAPTER **2**

Retail and
Data Analytics

This chapter provides an in-depth look into the collection, storage, and uses of retailer data. It includes a broad explanation of the terms frequently used in the information technology (IT) areas when discussing point of sale (POS) systems. This chapter also introduces you to a wide variety of examples and case studies of real projects that I have developed over time. These projects demonstrate the heavy reliance on data and the power of analytics to make use of it.

HARD-CORE DATA TERMS: NOW WE'RE TALKING ABOUT THE FUN STUFF

Again, knowing the correct vocabulary for the audience you are speaking to is critical. In most retail IT areas, these terms are common. And remember, the IT departments usually hold the keys to the data, so being able to speak their language is a must.

- *Header files, detail files, tender files.* See the "Market Basket" section for a detailed explanation of each of these file types.
- *Item cross-reference files.* These are the master lists of all item number combinations.
- *Merchandise ordering processing system (MOPS).* MOPS uses POS sales data to generate a reorder of an item that has been sold. This is the replenishment system.

■ *Register types (IBM, Fujitsu, NCR, etc.).* Each type of register has its own operating system.

■ *Tender type.* Typically cash, check, charge, and debit are the standard payment types.

■ *Transaction log (TLOG) files.* The TLOG is the beginning of market basket data, and contains header, detail, and tender files.

Makes sense, right? Sure it does, with a little help.

MARKET BASKET

Market basket data is typically brought into the retailer through files known as *TLOG*. This is the raw data feed that comes from the POS register, and it is most often stored on a relational database. The data is built in three sections: the header, the detail, and the tender.

1. The header data will include store number, register number, operator number, beginning date, and time of transaction. These will all be data points to identify where and when the transaction occurred. At Kmart, working within the confines of privacy laws, we also left a range of space to collect additional data from the consumer (zip code, phone number, etc.).

2. The detail data will include universal product code (UPC) number, price type, sale type, quantity, and actual price at which each item is sold.

3. The tender data will include tender type (e.g., cash, check, charge, and coupon), check number, charge number, debit number, level 1 and 2 data from the magnetic stripe ("mag-stripe"), and approval codes. The mag-stripe typically has three levels of data embedded in it. Depending on the card reader the retailer is using (usually one from Symbol Technologies), he may not be able to use the data stored there. This section will also include the end time stamp of the transaction, which makes it easier to quantify the amount of time each transaction takes. Retailers such as Walmart put great emphasis on the transaction time.

Note that the stock-keeping unit (SKU) and item description are not included within the TLOG data stream. All retailers use an item description cross-reference table. This table includes all UPC numbers and each one's associated SKU number, as well as the item description, list price, package quantity, and all other descriptors. This method avoids replication of data across the tables where it is stored, and saves time and space. Kmart used a system called MOPS (merchandise order processing system). It kept all the item numbers, SKU numbers, and merchandise orders organized. All retailers have this type of system, and the data that is kept here is crucial when discussing market basket use. UPC numbers without the item numbers and item descriptions are just a bunch of numbers; you would have no chance of finding any relationship between the baskets or products.

DATA STORAGE 101

Retailers today collect data from many sources, including in-store registers, online transactions, online search engines, and third-party providers. Grocery stores today track consumers' every move with devices ranging from radio frequency identification (RFID) beacons on shopping carts and handheld price checkers to thermal scanners in the ceiling. Where do you put this data? And with the introduction of social media text mining, the amount of data collected will increase tenfold. Retailers today are using a variety of sophisticated storage devices, and the majority of retailers are using very large systems from IBM, Teradata, and Oracle.

The following is an overview of some of these databases and their designs:

- Retailers most often store their POS or market basket data on very large databases. Walmart, Kmart, Target, Meijer, and most other large international retailers will be using the NCR Teradata Massively Parallel Processor (MPP) or IBM's DB2 structure. In smaller retailer environments, the database of choice is either the IBM AS400 or Oracle Sun Microsystems.

- Whatever the choice, these databases all use relational models in their architecture (relational database modeling structure, or RDMS). When you are collecting every item within every transaction, the amount of data can quickly grow enormous.

■ For MPP-type relational databases, there are two basic designs: normalized and denormalized. There are pros and cons for both depending on your access (query) method and your load (input) method. The following are the primary differences between these two methods:

  ■ Denormalized table designs will have many fewer tables, but these tables will be larger, with many more fields. Because there are fewer tables, the complexity of the joins and indexes between the tables should be simpler to build and maintain. The ideal design for a denormalized structure would be one large table (very much oversimplified, but used as an example). Because there are fewer tables, the chance for data contention grows considerably. Data contention simply means that every query is fighting for the same data point within the same table. Also, when loading data, you have to freeze the whole table while it is being updated, which means locking out all queries until the update is completed. These designs are not the best for analysts because the queries can run for a long time.

  ■ Normalized designs will have many more tables, with many fewer data fields within each one. Efficient indexing is required, as there will be many more keys to join each table together. An index (key field) is simply the same data field within multiple tables, which allows you to join tables together (that is, make it appear as though they are one big table). Table updates are much quicker to accomplish and there are fewer contention issues.

■ There are also databases known as mirrors, or copies of the original. These mirrors receive updates during the day and will be switched over to the primary database at some scheduled time. The goal is two-fold: to have a backup database, and to have less contention between queries and updating. The queries always point to the primary, while the mirror is receiving updates.

At Kmart, we followed the normalized relational database philosophy and managed as many as 35 tables for marketing alone. The largest table held the market basket detail, and had over 10 billion rows of data. We used a Teradata Join Index, commonly referred to as virtual indexing. When a query touched one of the larger tables, the indexing was automatically invoked. These methods accelerated queries by ensuring that the correct tables were joined consistently. Always include the database administrators in any database development projects. They are worth their weight in gold.

We held data from both online (Bluelight.com, Kmart.com) and all brick-and-mortar stores. Because we could find ways to join this data, we were able to better understand our consumers' preferences. One problem with accelerating online purchasing for many retailers is the lost revenue from in-store impulse buying, which adds significant margins. Impulse buying can be established online and takes special planning, but the rewards can be enormous. Because we could blend the data, we were able to identify those consumers who consistently selected a particular brand or product type both online and in-store. With this information, we could target market through e-mail with one-to-one offers. This is just one clear advantage of database management.

DATA WITHOUT USE IS OVERHEAD

This is a statement I heard many years ago, and have been using ever since. It speaks to the cost of storing data without gaining any market share or adding any sales volume to the mix. If a retailer is serious about gaining market share, decreasing the cost of goods sold, or increasing sales while decreasing interchange fees, then sharing this data with its strategic partners, like Global Decision Sciences, is very worthwhile. To be successful, you have to receive some value add from the data that you store. In today's environment, with so many sources of free streaming data, you have to be extremely cautious in what you collect and store and what you discard. Sources like social media sites, Internet search engines, and phone networks all collect data at amazing rates, and the first instinct is to collect all of it, because it might be useful some day. The cost of storing the data is only half the problem; getting to the data when you need it and being able to analyze the data when you are ready to investigate it is a huge issue to tackle. All of these are costly and need to be taken into account when looking at the usefulness of the data.

Data is not a scary thing; in the right hands, it can produce a masterpiece. In the wrong hands, it can produce a real nightmare. Know what you want from it before you begin mining, or you may find yourself on an endless quest.

CASE STUDIES AND PRACTICAL EXAMPLES OF DATA-RELATED RETAIL PROJECTS

The projects discussed in the following sections have included many types of data. Be aware that POS and market basket are two very different levels of data, and should be used accordingly. For each example, I provide the project name and a short description of what the project entailed. Although these are real examples, always be creative in your approach to solving business needs. I delve into deeper levels of analytics later in the book.

Try to not just solve problems but find workable solutions, and always look for the hidden insights that only robust analytics can deliver. Also remember that the ability to solve issues and develop solutions that are easily understood and implemented will be more appreciated by business. Developing complicated mathematical solutions just for the sake of looking complex can backfire. The possibilities are endless.

Trade Area Modeling

A trade area (TA) is simply the area around your store where the majority of your consumers come from. These trade areas can be many shapes and sizes, depending on many factors. If you are in a heavily populated area, the TA can be small, while in sparsely populated areas the TA would be large. Designate the polygon area around each store location that would encompass the majority of a store's frequent shopper base. The data for this level of analytics is frequently latitude and longitude, but it is more easily collected at the zip code level. Many people will use the less accurate method of rings or circles to show the circumference around a store. This method can work, but can also be very inaccurate when bringing competitor data into the analysis. One of the important uses of TA analysis is including your competitor's locations, and identifying what effect if any they are having on your consumer base. Many grocery retailers use a method called gravity modeling, which simply means weighting the population on the basis of their likelihood to shop one location over another. Detailed retail TA modeling market basket level data is a requirement. The art and science of mapping are discussed in a later section.

Real Estate Site Selection Modeling

There are many uses for the trade areas once they are defined. One use is helping real estate marketers identify or drill down to areas of opportunity. With a map of all penetration from the existing trade areas, it is easy to visually represent the geography where the store coverage is weakest. It is also easy to show where your competitors are most likely to evaluate space for a new store. Your analysis should take into account many different types of data and methods of analytics. The most important starting point is determining the similarities of the complete existing store base (market basket affinities is one of the most critical components), along with store size, open date, population, and ethnicity. Typically you would include the top 11 data points (metrics) in your statistics model. Once the model has been completed, it is easy to group (cluster) the stores together based on their similarities. The stores that make up a given cluster are referred to as sister stores. After grouping, you take the latitude and longitude of the proposed site and match it to the nearest cluster to forecast the future potential of the new site. Although a high-level analysis, this should provide you with a general understanding.

At Kmart, we were able to cut the new store breakeven from six years to two years because we were able to avoid the selection of bad sites. We were also able to develop smaller store formats to fit into the neighborhood-type malls. One of the unexpected benefits of this process was the ability to deliver a much more refined grand opening start-up merchandise mix. We were able to cut millions of dollars from the initial setup by better understanding the needs of the local consumer base. Again, by utilizing data from multiple existing stores, modeling them against the new site profile, and projecting the site's two-, three-, and four-year population growth, we could afford to build on a site that previously would have been thought too risky.

Competitor Threat Analytics

Competition in the retail marketplace is becoming more of a threat every day, as the marketplace continues to shrink and the competitive environment becomes more of a concern for many retailers. Understanding where your business fits within this ever-changing marketplace is sometimes called retail trade area analytics. Trade area analytics is becoming more complex and businesses are becoming more reliant on the study of competitive threat analytics. The basics behind trade areas reside in mapping or geographic information systems (GIS) tools.

The following are some different types of trade areas and how they are generated, including an explanation of how they are developed:

- You will need all latitude and longitude data points for all your stores as well as those from the competitors you are evaluating. Latitude and longitude are data points that are derived from an address. Many companies can provide geographic plot data (geocoded) from a set of addresses. Some companies use data from ESRI, which has developed a tool called ArcInfo. This is one of the strongest and most widely used GIS tools in the industry; another very widely used tool is MapInfo. Either one is a good choice. They both use layers as a base for displaying very intricate and complicated information.

- The primary emphasis is to determine how many customers are in a general proximity (trade area) that could be assigned to both the competitor and the primary retailer (overlapping trade area). For new-entry competitors, you can estimate which customer zip codes or addresses will be most affected by the new entry. You then have to determine what percentage of the customers' spend will stay and how much will transfer to the new site. You then target market the households between the two sites with relevant offers to keep them shopping at your store.

- Transfer sales analysis can also be useful when a retailer opens a new store that overlaps with the existing store's trade area. Transfer sales data refers to the percentage of sales that will go to the new store once it opens. There can also be lost sales analysis, which focuses on the percentage of customers' spend that will go to the competitor. Transfer sales analysis is a critical piece in the new site sales analysis and breakeven forecasting.

Walmart is the master of this model. It is constantly opening stores that overlap existing stores' trade areas. The impact on this strategy at a store level can be confusing, as each existing store will perform slightly worse, but the magic comes from the incremental lift that all stores combined can bring. This process can also effectively lock out competition from encroaching on the territory. This was a strong tactic in the late 1990s and into the mid-2000s. But the entry of the neighborhood markets and smaller footprint stores will open this strategy to new areas.

Merchandise Mix Modeling: Combining Multiple Data Sources

Merchandise mix modeling means tailoring the mix of merchandise to each store's specific consumer base. There are many tools available today to help retailers assign the best mix of merchandise (SpaceMan from ACNielsen, Intactix, SAS, and more). All of these tools rely heavily on the market basket level of detail. Defining the shelf space that is available for specific brands of merchandise is critical. Using the data to determine what merchandise is selling together (affinities) and where the households that shop the store are located can define your mix at the individual store level. This process of blending the right merchandise with the right group of stores is called store demand modeling.

The following example illustrates how complex this process really is. Merchants, for the most part, see mix modeling as placing the right product in the right store. The shelf- and space-management department sees it as just placing these products on the appropriate shelf where they fit best. Real estate managers, those individuals who buy parcels of land for new stores, look for population size to support total store sales growth goals. As you can see, very few areas take the whole picture into perspective. The analytics team plays an important role in keeping a holistic view of all parts of the process. We are the ones who bring each of the separate pieces into an organized analytics framework. The business outcome can be a reduced amount of slow-selling merchandise along with an increase in the best SKUs, which increases sales and revenue. All of this occurs on a store-by-store basis.

Exhibit 2.1 is an example of the store demand process flow.

Market basket analytics (MBA) uses the data that comes in from each store to model the particular patterns of behavior for both merchandise and frequency. Credit and loyalty data can help in building consumer clusters of similar groups. Shopper insights are the most difficult and least tangible inputs to gather. However, they are some of the most useful if collected and analyzed correctly. Store location should be the easiest and most accurate data point collected. Geographic and demographic data are the easiest points to include in a mapping utility and can be some of the most relevant insights to your models.

The difficult part is selecting the right metric to group the stores correctly. I have found that most people start with geodemographics to build store models, which makes sense on the surface. But, shopping behavior and store location data (store size, selling square footage, season code, and so on) are equally if not more important. When selecting the best mix of merchandise for a given store, use the similar store characteristics; that is, sister stores. Sister stores are stores that display very similar characteristics for metrics such as sales, total store square footage size, and number of departments.

The following examples highlight two quick benefits that can be realized by developing this store-clustering model.

1. Retailers need to maintain a high turnover rate for their merchandise to ensure they are selling a single SKU many times before the freight bill arrives. So having the right SKU on hand, in the right quantity (and in the right store), is critical. Most grocery chains will have an average margin of 4 percent to 5 percent turnover, which does not give much room for error in picking what mix to carry. If the product sits on the counter

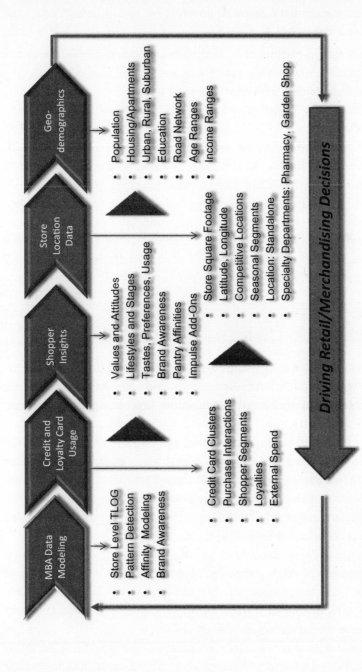

MBA Data Modeling
- Store Level TLOG
- Pattern Detection
- Affinity Modeling
- Brand Awareness

Credit and Loyalty Card Usage
- Credit Card Clusters
- Purchase Interactions
- Shopper Segments
- Loyalties
- External Spend

Shopper Insights
- Values and Attitudes
- Lifestyles and Stages
- Tastes, Preferences, Usage
- Brand Awareness
- Pantry Affinities
- Impulse Add-Ons

Store Location Data
- Store Square Footage
- Latitude, Longitude
- Competitive Locations
- Seasonal Segments
- Location: Standalone
- Specialty Departments: Pharmacy, Garden Shop

Geo-demographics
- Population
- Housing/Apartments
- Urban, Rural, Suburban
- Education
- Road Network
- Age Ranges
- Income Ranges

Driving Retail/Merchandising Decisions

Exhibit 2.1 Building Customer Insights through Intelligent Data Capture

and does not sell before the freight bill arrives, the retailer will have to pay out of his profit.

2. A strong benefit of this method is in the logistics of the distribution centers. If similar stores are grouped together (clusters or sister store methodology) a single truck can drop off merchandise to many stores on a single delivery from the distribution center (DC). This saves considerable time and money, because the trucks do not have to drive back to the DC for the next store's merchandise. Walmart has perfected this method by building DCs around a geographic and demographics base. Then they build their stores around the DC, and build the mix of merchandise by using each store's market basket data to drive replenishment. They make it seem easy, but it takes high-powered databases and many terabytes of data.

CELEBRITY MARKETING: TRACKING EFFECTIVENESS

Kmart had a department within the marketing division that was dedicated to managing celebrity relationships and contracts. We had many celebrities who represented our business. The group also included many sports figures.

Most of the celebrities represented a line of merchandise that was tailored to their own line of goods or one that Kmart had selected for them. One celebrity had by far the largest line of merchandise; she actually had her own line of home goods, outdoor patio, hardware, soft home, and more. She helped with the launch of our new bench-top power tools and accessories.

During the grand opening of one of our stores, this celebrity, along with a number of others, attended to help bring in a large crowd. In this case, I was assisting the celebrity in the hardware section, where she was taking note of all the equipment on the counters, paying particular attention to the bench-top tools.

When the store opened, the consumers would line up to get autographs from their favorite celebrity. For this opening, the line to see this celebrity was extremely long. She stood there for over two hours answering consumers' questions about everything from power tools to paint colors. She answered every question and didn't leave until the last consumer had the chance to see her.

I bring up this story because at Kmart, the analytics team was responsible for monitoring the incremental increase in quantity and sales of each item associated with a particular celebrity. It was part of our responsibility to work with the promotions department to get a schedule of appearances for each celebrity. Based on this visit and many more like it, we could track the incremental sales of hardware products back to this celebrity's visits.

When another celebrity appeared on a late-night talk show, she always made a mention of her line of clothes (available at Kmart). We tracked these products and very often were able to show an incremental increase in sales shortly after the event.

At this time, Kmart also sponsored both IndyCar and NASCAR teams. We tracked the regions (states and cities) where races were to occur and measured any licensed merchandise sales around the track before, during, and after the races. We always saw an increase in sales from the NASCAR fans, but had a tougher time tracking the IndyCar series. We believed the Kmart shopper was more of a NASCAR fan, and shopped at Kmart for pre-race gear. We also tracked all the brands that were mentioned on the sponsored car itself. Each location on the NASCAR car had a different cost associated with it. The prominent locations, like on the hood or the back bumper, cost the most because these would be seen more clearly by people in the television audience. Again, part of our responsibility was validating that the different locations on the car were producing incremental increases of sale for each product. This was tough, but through many different experiments we found a way to validate it with good results.

Tracking was difficult to measure since so many factors can influence the movement of merchandise. So correct timing was an absolute must, along with tracking the correct line of merchandise.

We found that certain late night talk shows delivered more incremental sales to Kmart than others, and certain racetrack venues produced a far superior sales increase.

During one race, a pit crew was photographed using the Kmart bench-top tools and sprays. This photograph was distributed by one of the racing magazines, and produced a fabulous spike in sales for the bench-top line. These are the times that make celebrity marketing worthwhile.

HOUSE BRAND VERSUS NAME BRAND

When developing a tiered approach to pricing, it is critical to maintain some parity in pricing between house brands and the brand name counterpart. As an example, Folgers Coffee's three-pound bag may be priced at $10.00, while the house brand's best may be priced at $7.00.

This percentage parity must be maintained across all the brands, and continued through the sizes. A 10-pound bag of coffee should cost slightly less than twice the cost of a 5-pound bag of coffee. For example, 10 pounds of coffee would cost $10.00, while 5 pounds would cost $6.50; thus the 10-pound bag is a better deal.

This helps show the value of bulk buying. There are many software packages that can help you develop and maintain these price parity levels, but the majority of these packages relate only to commodity and consumable products.

The move to increase margins has spawned many different types of house brands: lightbulbs, house cleaners, mops, apparel, pots, and pans, and more. These types of general merchandise categories do not fit in very well with many of the price management software products.

Purchase frequency is one of the key attributes to set a realistic price parity quotient. Without a fairly frequent purchase cycle, these software products can become erratic.

At Kmart, we used Priceman from ACNielsen for our supercenter grocery products with good success. However, we developed our own pricing algorithms for the general merchandise categories. We also took into account the movement of the products from 30-inch end caps to the larger 90-inch end caps. These were the ends of a longer aisle counter, and generally produced far higher sales than the standard side counter locations.

These merchandise locations had to be included within our analytics and price modeling process as the volume in sales was a lengthy calculation with many months of sales points.

E-BUSINESS: CLICKS AND MORTAR

There has been a dramatic growth in the e-business channel recently. Many retailers have witnessed the explosion of sales, which has accelerated their desire to gain an online presence. While online business can be seen as a valued channel, it also presents a new and sometimes difficult dilemma for information systems and analytics. How do you account for a consumer's preference to shop online while there are brick-and-mortar stores to shop at? Does your organization want more online sales with a cannibalization from your existing stores? Measuring success within the e-business sector can be difficult but is not impossible.

Cross-channel analytics is seeing a huge area of expansion right now. This involves joining all of the online transaction and consumer data with the in-store transaction and consumer data. This sounds easy, but it can be extremely difficult to do. To accomplish this, you need to develop a customer relationship management (CRM) infrastructure that can distinguish each shopper's identity. This can be developed at the numeric level, such as the credit-card or debit-card level, where the same card is used for both online and in-store transactions. The best way to accomplish this is to go through the efforts of building your customer database with all identifiable fields included. This can be accomplished from the online side using ship-to–bill-to data along with the customer's name.

The key to a successful cross-channel strategy is to build a centralized repository that includes all customer information. Within this database, you need to distinguish the channel-of-acquisition and channel-of-purchase preferences. Again, this can be accomplished only by tying in the sales and transaction databases from both online and in-store activity. These are called dependencies and are critical for a good strategic marketing plan. Since online businesses use these databases at a daily activity level, it is important to keep the data organized very efficiently.

One big advantage to developing a cross-channel database is the ability to cross-sell to individual consumers by understanding what they choose to purchase online (big items that can be delivered to the house) versus products they tend to buy in-store (groceries, apparel, everyday needs). Knowing this helps retailers design the most effective marketing programs. My team developed a cross-channel/cross-merchandise marketing structure in the United States and pushed it a step further by marketing to those consumers that tended to shop only online with offers that were only good in-store. The advantage is that once a customer is in the store, the opportunity to sell impulse items goes up dramatically. It is much more difficult to get online consumers to impulse buy, and if they do, it is nearly impossible to identify which items are bought on impulse. We spent significant time trying to develop models to predict the best merchandise to present to each consumer at the time of purchase. Once we knew which products had been placed in the online basket and presented at the checkout screen, we tried to make additional offers before the final purchase. Sometimes these worked, but it was mostly by chance.

The online business landscape is becoming more crowded and competitive every day. To be successful will take a lot of effort. The following is a short list of important points to keep in mind as you begin thinking about whether to build an online presence.

- Expect continued blurring of the clicks and brick-and-mortar walls. This phenomenon is quickly gaining momentum and is becoming a major strategic initiative. There are retailers now that do not even have walls, existing only in the virtual space of a web site (for example, Amazon.com).

  In 1999, Victoria's Secret ran a promotion during the Super Bowl that drove more than 1.5 million hits to their web site in less than 30 minutes. In 2000, they delivered a fashion show online that drove well over 2.5 million hits. Their online sales have grown from $0 in 1998 to over $200 million in 2001. Their web site allows parent company Limited Brands to display a much wider variety of merchandise to a far broader audience. But they have no illusions of eliminating the brick building.

- Apparel mall shops have been building collective databases of online shoppers as well as brick shoppers and developing a new communication strategy that can drive Web shoppers to the store and give store shoppers a personalized shopping experience online. These e-mail libraries are now being developed to increase the stores' ability to effectively target market catalogues online.

- It is becoming increasingly important to collect e-mail addresses at every possible consumer touchpoint. Of equal importance is the maintenance of these addresses. Be aware that people have on average 3.5 e-mail addresses, and tend to use only one for their personal business. Many switch addresses two or three times a year, so the hygiene of this database will be a necessity. Kmart, working within the confines of privacy laws, had millions of pingable e-mail addresses. These addresses were considered a prized asset. The term *pingable* simply means that the account is active and can receive messages through e-mail.

Traditional Web analytics looked only at click-stream performance, while many companies are now moving into Internet customer management (CM). CM provides the foundation for optimizing your online business and marketing decisions through the process of combining unique features of Web data with traditional Web analytics techniques—basically applying tried and true analytics methods to the unique world of the Internet. A process to build up your Internet analytics performance is listed next. This has worked for me in various retail and nonretail environments.

One approach that I have used across different organizations and business types is a phased design to my analytics regime. In designing the best-suited web site, it is common to include red and green button tests with which you can monitor the number of hits or the number of times a consumer pressed that particular button to go forward. These are typically called champion/challenger tests, and they allow you to monitor the results from each candidate.

Within each phase, the complexity of the work becomes increasingly difficult. When you include consumer data in the equation, you are actually tracking ship-to-bill-to data with any brick-and-mortar store information you have been able to collect. Many companies that subscribe to loyalty programs are able to combine online and in-store data using account numbers. The benefits to this process are numerous, including targeted marketing through e-mail.

Phase I: Web site optimization

- Use champion/challenger design of experiment (DOE) to optimize site functionality.
- Use regression and chi-square to test results.

Phase II: Combining customer data with site usage data

- Use champion/challenger DOE to optimize customer performance.
- Look at purchase behavior of consumers over time and build targeting campaigns specific to them. Hold out a control group as the challenger to use as a basis for comparison.

Phase III: E-servicing and e-cross-sell

- A business sector that could benefit from this process immediately and is best suited for Internet business is retail banking. Paperless statements are a key point, but the ability to up-sell and cross-sell through an Internet account is key to today's low-cost marketing structure. Balance transfer is one example of a cross-sell area.
- Using Internet applications and utilities to cross-sell additional products and services is a natural.

This phased approach can work equally well in the retail world, as you begin testing different break points in the transaction process. A break point is the point within a transaction at which the consumer abandons the basket. By applying some of these measurement processes, it is possible to isolate a particular pattern for which tests can be set up to determine why a consumer (or groups of consumers) would choose to stop shopping.

We developed simple steps called green button–red button, in which two different tests were run using two sets of parameters. Each test was well controlled, and the data for each set was also closely controlled. By doing many controlled tests, even in the Internet space we were able to quickly identify those points within the transaction process when consumers felt unsure of how to continue. In the end, we found that the final step, in which we ask about payment method, was worded poorly, and once this was corrected, the closure increased.

The statistical software company SAS has a strong set of utilities within its SAS Enterprise Miner that we used heavily.

AFFINITY MERCHANDISING: MERCHANDISE CROSS-SELL CASE STUDY

Affinity merchandising is the art and science of identifying those products that appear most often in the same basket. Another more complicated version is identifying the products that are purchased by the same consumer over time. At the simplest level, you can hang candy in the cosmetics department, so as the mom passes by with her kids in the cart they grab the candy. At the other end of the spectrum, you can go so far as to redesign the department layouts inside a store.

Based on how people shop and the affinities of the merchandise that they buy, we were able to determine the best departments to place next to each other on the sales floor. Traditionally there has been very little diversity in how stores are laid out, and there has been very little change in the past 20 years. In our White Lake test, we were able to define five cubes in the store in which merchandise was placed based on its frequency of purchase (cross-sell affinities). The basic idea was to reduce the amount of time shoppers had to hunt for their merchandise, which increased their time to browse for impulse items. The final store design resulted in a 20 percent increase in sales with a 22 percent reduction in the number of items being carried.

In Australia, I was able to develop a specific set of tools that depended heavily on SAS Enterprise Miner. One of the tools was developed to work specifically on market basket data to identify not only the affinity products that were purchased together most often, but also the seasonality of the combination. During the four seasons, we found different sets of merchandise with the highest affinity combinations.

The market basket data that retailers collect is simply a reflection of the register receipt (see Exhibit 2.2). Each SKU on the receipt is stored as a line item or row on the market basket table, within a transaction. Exhibit 2.2 is a copy of a traditional receipt.

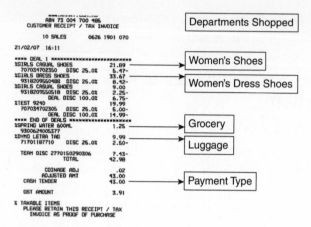

Retail Analytics Begins with the Sale

Exhibit 2.2 POS Receipt

This data is aggregated to the payment type for many analytics exercises, and that is the level I used here. I was able to use the co-branded credit card information from the retailer, along with all of the other credit card numbers, to build an affinity model. Affinity models look at all product associations and how these products are purchased together (or alone). As you find more of the product associations, you can begin to recognize behaviors and patterns. One of methods we use to detect these patterns is to use time series data, with which you can track a particular reference number, account number, or group of account numbers to measure the variability across a period of time (weeks, months, or seasons). This is different from looking at data for a specific time, like a single transaction.

There are different levels of market basket analytics.

Loyalty marketing:

- Can reduce unnecessary promotions to a mass target

- Can help determine which segments produce the highest return

- Allows you to target geographies instead of blanket marketing

- Can identify the 30 percent of accounts that generate 70 percent of profit

In retailing, market basket analysis can:

- Improve margins by eliminating unnecessary markdowns and promotions
- Determine which items to place together (build impulse)
- Suggest new store layouts to optimize basket size
- Identify brand loyalties (Pepsi, Coke, Kraft, Evian, Perrier)

The preceding list highlights the difference that data and analytics can make in identifying retail opportunities. In later chapters, I delve deeper into the field of loyalty marketing as well as demonstrate how using analytics and data mining properly can identify tremendous margin and cost-saving opportunities.

One of the most important lessons I have learned over the past 30 years of retail and analytics is that an analyst without a retail background can get you only so far and a retailer without an analytics background can be dangerous playing with data. A true master of the retail analytics science needs both backgrounds to fully understand what to look for in the data and to recognize when an opportunity presents itself. Being able to apply different statistical methods for specific uses can help uncover when the opportunity is big or huge.

MARKET BASKET ANALYSIS: EXAMPLES

The following are a few real examples of affinity reports that were developed and used across multiple continents for various retailers.

In the first example (see Exhibit 2.3), we were able to collect the transactions for a full year and evaluate the products purchased together most often. In this case, we see everyday wrap (gift wrap) is purchased 57 percent of the time when everyday cards are purchased. Since this is a fairly well-known combination, it is a good test of logic. The real magic comes from being able to mathematically identify how the patterns fit if the customers purchase cards first. The combination falls off to 26.82 percent.

The comment in Exhibit 2.3 regarding margin management is heavily supported by the fact that women will (69 percent of the time)

Some particularly strong relationships (affinity strengths) are shown

# TRANS.	Merchandise Relationships	# Trans. Primary	# Trans. Affinity	Affinity Strength	Penetration	Lift
733,585	EVERYDAY WRAP ==> EVERYDAY CARDS	1,295,095	2,734,731	56.64%	1.29%	11.78
733,585	EVERYDAY CARDS ==> EVERYDAY WRAP	2,734,731	1,295,095	26.82%	1.29%	11.78
627,415	BOTTOMS – OUTERWEAR ==> TOPS – OUTERWEAR	901,041	1,293,799	69.63%	1.10%	30.62
627,415	TOPS – OUTERWEAR ==> BOTTOMS – OUTERWEAR	1,293,799	901,041	48.49%	1.10%	30.62
327,706	COMPACT DISC ==> VIDEO DVD	1,560,498	3,420,898	21.00%	0.58%	3.49
303,817	BRIEFS ==> SOCKS	924,992	1,633,417	32.85%	0.53%	11.44
151,302	PACKAGED ==> NOVELTY – EASTER	397,979	451,275	38.02%	0.27%	47.93
151,302	NOVELTY – EASTER ==> PACKAGED	451,275	397,979	33.53%	0.27%	47.93
148,566	GIRLS TOPS ==> GIRLS BOTTOMS	331,021	488,456	44.88%	0.26%	52.28
130,370	CAR CHEMICALS ==> CLEANING/AIR FRESH	407,278	460,320	32.01%	0.23%	39.57
125,863	SEEDLINGS ==> OUTDOOR PLANTS	398,139	673,835	31.61%	0.22%	26.69
124,833	MULTIEGG PACK ==> NOVELTY – EASTER	292,119	451,275	42.73%	0.22%	53.88
116,656	MULTIEGG PACK ==> PACKAGED	292,119	397,979	39.93%	0.21%	57.09
94,052	COMBOS ==> TACKLE ACCESSORIES	169,248	729,682	55.57%	0.17%	43.33

One year of data was provided.

There are 200,000,000 SKU level records and 71,000,000 transaction level records (i.e., baskets).

Observation: Insights build margin management
If a customer purchases BOTTOMS, 69% of the time he or she will also purchase TOPS.

If a customer purchases EVERYDAY WRAP, 57% of the time he or she will also purchase EVERYDAY CARDS.

Takeaway – Do not promote bottoms with tops, they are purchased together anyway! This will eliminate significant margin erosion.

Exhibit 2.3 Market Basket Analysis: Full-Year Perspective

purchase both slacks and tops together within the same transaction. Since these items are frequently purchased together, it is unwise to promote both at the same time. You can make up significant margin by placing these two items together but discounting only one or the other.

One big insight that the retailer found was the ability to cross-merchandise unrelated products. I am sure you have seen products hanging from hooks alongside merchandise that does not seem to relate very well. There is a science to this and it can be very profitable. Does the term *impulse items* ring a bell?

This type of affinity analysis can be hugely instrumental to space and shelf management systems. Being able to model unrelated products within a plot plan helps you design where and how you want the merchandise presented. I relied heavily on this method while developing new store and shelf layouts across many retail formats from different countries, including Puerto Rico, Australia, the United Kingdom, and China. One big find was the ability to identify those products that could be bundled together and sold at a discount. Although the total price was reduced slightly, the additional quantity that we sold made up significant profits.

In Exhibit 2.4, you can see that the affinity analysis was developed using time series data, and that we were able to break out each season from the total year to determine how merchandise was purchased differently.

Again, we see the same relationships in the everyday cards and gift wrap as well as the tops outerwear and bottoms outerwear, although finding indoor and outdoor plants together at that volume was a surprise.

In the case of indoor and outdoor plants, the two categories of merchandise were displayed in two different areas, making it difficult for the consumer to find them. We redesigned the floor space to make an adjacent display that placed the two categories closer together, which heavily increased the sales. We also cross-merchandised more of the accessories that carry a higher margin, like potting soil and growth sticks.

Again, some of these affinities seem obvious once you see them in an analysis, but to the merchant and those responsible for store

Some particularly strong relationships (affinity strengths) are shown

# TRANS.	Merchandise Relationships	# Trans. Primary	# Trans. Affinity	Affinity Strength	Penetration	Lift
184,427	BOTTOMS – OUTERWEAR ==> TOPS – OUTERWEAR	263,336	325,672	70.03%	1.26%	31.53
209,075	EVERYDAY WRAP ==> EVERYDAY CARDS	352,950	752,556	59.24%	1.43%	11.54
184,427	TOPS – OUTERWEAR ==> BOTTOMS – OUTERWEAR	325,672	263,336	56.63%	1.26%	31.53
35,271	SHORTS – BOTTOMS ==> KNIT TOPS – BOYS TOPS	75,123	105,876	46.95%	0.24%	65.02
38,555	GIRLS TOPS ==> GIRLS BOTTOMS	83,933	134,856	45.94%	0.26%	49.94
34,146	SHORTS – BOTTOMS ==> KNIT TOPS – TOPS	83,804	149,799	40.75%	0.23%	39.88
37,959	INDOOR PLANTS ==> OUTDOOR PLANTS	109,275	219,301	34.74%	0.26%	23.22
35,271	KNIT TOPS – BOYS TOPS ==> SHORTS – BOTTOMS	105,876	75,123	33.31%	0.24%	65.02
33,482	CAR CHEMICALS ==> CLEANING/AIR FRESH	103,105	120,513	32.47%	0.23%	39.51
72,383	BRIEFS ==> SOCKS	229,611	381,140	31.52%	0.49%	12.13
47,834	EVERYDAY SPECIALTY ==> EVERYDAY CARDS	154,685	752,556	30.92%	0.33%	6.02
35,807	KNIT TOPS – TOPS ==> SHORTS – BOTTOMS	119,724	93,799	29.91%	0.24%	46.75
46,519	SEEDLINGS ==> OUTDOOR PLANTS	160,178	219,301	29.04%	0.32%	19.42
53,186	LICENSED STATIONERY ==> ART & GRAPHICS	185,607	490,620	28.66%	0.36%	8.56
38,555	GIRLS BOTTOMS ==> GIRLS TOPS	134,856	83,933	28.59%	0.26%	49.94

Observation:

Plant categories (INDOOR PLANTS and OUTDOOR PLANTS) have stronger relationships in spring.
There is a great opportunity to merchandise related products (growth sticks and potting soil) with higher margins.

Exhibit 2.4 Seasonal Basket Analysis: Spring

38

alignments, these facts make a big difference. It is not easy to redesign space or move merchandise around the store, since for every move there is another product that requires a new home.

A case in point was in the evaluation of the cooking oil category. The retailer wanted to eliminate one SKU to make room for a better-selling product (SKU rationalization). The typical way to do this would have been to rank each SKU within the category and then eliminate the slowest, lowest-volume item from within the category.

Before we made this move, we pulled all the basket data for each product to determine which item was in the largest baskets, from our most important consumers. We had previously determined that the 20 percent rule applied, as these consumers produced 70 percent of the profit base. We did not want to eliminate an item that our top-tier consumer base purchased.

The analytics team was able to identify the affinity groups that each SKU within the category belonged to. It is important to determine the cross-category purchasing from each SKU. This score goes into the decision-making process of what stays and what goes. In simple category management, the performance of each SKU within the category is ranked on a sales–quantity sold–frequency basis, but never on the basis of the product's ability to attract buyers, its likelihood of being included in high-quantity baskets, or its relationship to other products outside of its category.

In today's SKU rationalization (SKU and product reductions from assortment), it is not enough to simply rank products based on performance. A more complex comparison across categories and departments is required.

In the end, we were able to determine that the higher-priced product (olive oil, in this case) was by far the preferred product of our prime consumer group. We were able to identify which stores our prime consumers shopped at and found that the high-end oil was not carried in all stores, which was immediately corrected.

The sales of this product increased considerably and we kept our higher-margin consumers happy. We also did not eliminate the alternative product, but did reduce its facing.

We checked to make sure that reducing facing did not lead to an out-of-stock position, but this never occurred.

STORE DEPARTMENTAL CROSS-SELLING

One of the last steps in our market basket analysis example was to overlay the departmental affinities across a store layout to visually understand how the consumer shopped in a typical store. In this case, we identified heavy cross-shopping in the apparel side of the store. We put an affinity strength index on each relationship to keep the interconnectivity in perspective.

More than 30 percent of the shoppers who purchased infant accessories also purchased children's wear, both high-margin goods. Thirty percent of the consumers who purchased children's wear also purchased footwear and women's wear. An equal percentage of consumers who purchased women's underwear also purchased women's wear.

We observed a very strong affinity within the apparel area (as shown in Exhibit 2.5), much stronger than we had initially thought.

After I had presented this to the retailer, she informed me that over the previous six months, the store had totally redesigned the apparel area, at a cost of several million dollars, and that she had no idea whether the new design was working. Sure, she could see some lift in the individual departments, but she had no idea that the area was cross-shopped this heavily. She had never seen this affinity analysis before.

The retailer was also very surprised to see the low affinity score to the right half of the store. Shoppers were apparently not buying apparel and general merchandise together.

There are other business reasons for using this type of analytics. At Kmart, we frequently looked at specific product sales within a category. In this case, we wanted to know what products sold most often with paper towels, when they were on promotion and when they were not.

Paper towels do not have a high margin, and we felt that those products that sold with paper towels (in the same basket) were also low margin, but we had no proof. Our advertising department felt that advertising paper towels was a big consumer draw, and that we should also advertise associated products as well, since this could bring in more consumers. Our challenge was to develop an analysis that looked at the cross-sell affinities of this product.

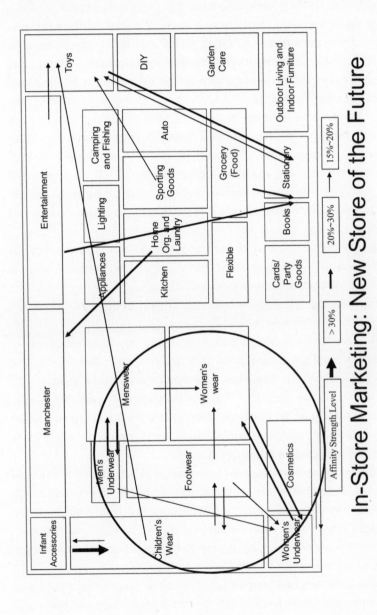

In-Store Marketing: New Store of the Future

Exhibit 2.5 Store Layout (Affinity Strength)

We applied this same method at a Kmart U.S. store with similar results. We developed the White Lake test, which was conducted at a smaller footprint store that did very well. We had tried to increase sales through many types of marketing initiatives like special signage, in-store banners, and area marketing. The store seemed to be at a cap in sales, but the population and demographics showed that we should have been able to grow.

We developed a plan to identify all of the primary cross-selling items (affinities) from the previous year's market basket data. This sounds like a huge data undertaking, but it was actually a very controlled data mining exercise. Our data was stored on one of the original Teradata databases, and we relied on our DBAs to govern the code. At that time, our market basket marketing database was several terabytes, and had billions of rows.

When I say we looked at the primary affinities, I mean that we did not look at every item from every transaction, but the highest occurrence of the same relationships. This means we were looking at those products that sold together most frequently across all departments.

This store was not a supercenter, so it did not have a full line of groceries, but did have the pantry area (for example, milk, bread, and other grocery staples). This made the data mining much easier.

Of equal importance was identifying those products that were purchased infrequently. Those products that were *not* being purchased on a regular basis and not being bought by our core shoppers were singled out for possible elimination.

One of the areas we needed to be careful of was the seasonal sales categories, such as Halloween, Christmas, and Valentine's Day. Along with these obvious categories, we needed to isolate the outdoor furniture and winter items (for example, snow shovels). These seasonal items could have a single day of seasonal time, whereas some categories could have weeks of shelf life.

These items are not carried as basic stock (carried all year), and the modeling we built needed to take this into account. All merchandise had a specific season code, and each of the products within the same season code was evaluated with a different model. This extra effort reduced the risk that we would incorrectly score the seasonal merchandise with the same measures as the basic merchandise. This also ensured that we could effectively identify the basic merchandise most frequently purchased with the seasonal goods. This single step was a huge win for the store plan-o-gram and buying-office departments. Up to this point, each area was evaluated in isolation, and we really did not know how the departments were cross-shopped during the holidays.

Because of this, we made much more effective use of flex space after the analytics. Flex space is the area of the sales floor that can be shared with seasonal goods without disturbing the placement of the regular merchandise.

Whenever you develop an analytics exercise of this magnitude, you invariably find something that you did not expect to find. In this case, the *aha* moment was the discovery of apparent zero matching. We actually found occurrences in which a relatively strong affinity between two products showed a sudden downward spike in performance. What was actually happening was that one of the two primary items was either out of stock, causing the models to produce warnings, or out of the bounds of measurement. We found a way to accurately predict a possible out-of-stock condition before a trigger figure was hit. Trigger figures are those numbers that alert you to place a reorder. Because POS replenishment is an automated process, it will help to avoid stockouts. There are always issues with automated replenishment, but today's systems are much more accurate than they were even five years ago.

Single Category Affinity Analysis: Paper Towels

The initial prompt for this analysis was the perception that the advertising department and the buying office were wasting significant marketing dollars by advertising affinity products together—in other words, advertising products together that would be naturally purchased together anyway. We would be losing margin by unnecessarily advertising such products.

The advertising department felt that the more we advertised, the more consumers would come in, and that we could make up any reduced margin in the volume we sold.

The buying merchandise group really didn't care what sold with their advertised category, as these products were from a different part of the organization (for example, consumer packaged goods and household cleaners), and any reduced margin did not hit their profit-and-loss statement. The chief marketing officer was the driver behind this analysis and understood that the corporation could save a great deal of margin while maintaining the traffic if we could better understand the dynamics.

For this exercise, we queried the database by pulling all baskets that contained paper towel SKUs, when they were sold on-ad (at a reduced price) and when they were sold at the regular price. We wanted to determine whether the products consumers purchased with paper towels differed when they were on-ad.

In this test, we were looking for the products purchased in the two scenarios to determine the most frequently purchased items when the paper towels were advertised at a discount. The paper towels were on promotion for several weeks and at their regular price for the same number of weeks.

When the paper towels were advertised, there were millions of baskets with the paper towels purchased. Of these baskets, the average number of items per basket was less than nine.

The top six most frequently purchased categories (affinity products) were:

1. Bath tissue, with the majority of these also purchased at reduced sale price

2. Laundry detergent, with a slight majority purchased on sale

3. Household cleaner, with less than a majority purchased on sale

4. Hand soap, with less than a majority purchased on sale

5. Paper plates, with less than a majority purchased on sale

6. Facial tissue, with a slight majority purchased on sale

There were millions of baskets with the paper towels purchased at their regular price. Of these baskets, the average number of items per basket was less than 10.

The top six affinity products were:

1. Bath tissue, with the majority also purchased at regular price
2. Household cleaner, with the majority purchased at regular price
3. Laundry detergent, with the majority purchased at regular price
4. Paper plates, with the majority purchased at regular price
5. Facial tissue, with the majority purchased at regular price
6. Hand soap, with the majority purchased at regular price

The end result of the analysis showed that there were common products purchased between the two periods (advertised and non-advertised) whether the paper towels were advertised or not.

- The majority of affinity items were purchased whether the paper towel was advertised or not.
- The top six items are identical. In fact, almost all of the top 100 items are the same on both lists.
- The total number of items per basket was slightly larger in the regular basket.
- The average basket total was identical.
- Products purchased when the paper towels were advertised were also predominantly on sale.

Consumers bought the same amount of paper towels whether on-ad or at the regular price. They purchased the same products at the same volume, but at full price when paper towels were not advertised. The big win was to not advertise strong affinity items at the same time as the primary product, paper towels in this case.

This single project saved us millions in unnecessary markdowns from just one category analyzed. We replicated this level of analysis across many of our commodity (lower margin) categories with similar savings.

Best Checkout Register Impulse Items for Christmas Season: Case Study

Our front-end registers were showing a decrease in the volume of impulse items being purchased in the weeks leading up to Christmas.

Christmas is the busiest shopping period in the year and we could not afford to lose any impulse sales, especially since these tended to be higher-margin sales.

I was asked to identify three key products that could be assigned to the checkout counter for November and December. The checkout counters are the most prized piece of real estate in the entire building. The items had to be small enough to hang on a peg hook and be available from existing stock. The checkout counters are approximately three feet long and four feet high, and do not have shelves.

Based on market basket analytics, I reviewed all the baskets from the previous year, as well as the most recent month's purchases, to identify current trends. I was able to identify those products that had little bearing on the other items in a basket (impulse), but high enough frequency to develop a pattern.

The thought was that if we could make it easier for the masses to find these items, our sales would increase dramatically. In the end, I identified disposable cameras, four-pack Scotch tape, and 12-pack double-A batteries. Again, the stock for these items came from merchandise on hand; no additional quantities were purchased.

The final tally showed millions of dollars in incremental sales gains. We were able to substantiate this total from the previous sell-through amounts from previous years, as well as the change in control and test stores. Not all stores had made the change to the checkout counter. This was a data-intensive exercise that proved to be extremely successful.

The business benefits included the following:

- A national incremental sales increase of millions of dollars year over year was realized.
- The increase was validated against control stores.
- No additional inventory was required.

In the next chapter, I concentrate on the apparel business model. Chapter 3 goes to the heart of retailing in a very fast-paced business, where data and analytics can save you from a considerable number of needless markdowns.

CHAPTER **3**

The Apparel
Industry

C hapter 2 attempted to bring the reader some basic level of knowledge of the retailer language. It included some examples and case studies of various projects in which data was a key enabler.

In this chapter, I provide more background on the origins of the apparel business and how it is managed. I then dive a little deeper into the usage of data in various scenarios as it relates to the apparel business. This chapter looks at issues and opportunities from a retailer's perspective.

I have had apparel partners from both ends of the retail spectrum: mass and specialty. I will touch on both of these businesses after first describing the apparel business overall.

I selected apparel because it has some of the most dramatic extremes in cycle times (seasons) for both replenishment and markdowns. Both of these factors are data intensive for merchants, and will offer a unique perspective and set of challenges.

MANY TYPES OF APPAREL BUSINESSES

There are many types of apparel businesses, from the rough textiles (raw materials) to the very high-end New York and Milan haute couture. I will touch on many examples, but will apply more focus in this book to the mass merchandiser and mass apparel (for example, The Limited and Gap) types of businesses.

The typical mass merchandiser is a store that sells apparel and household goods as well as groceries, such as Walmart, Kmart, or Target. A mass apparel retailer would be a store like Kohl's, Gap, or a chain brand like The Limited. This type of retailer sticks to clothing, but will also carry many fashion accessories and shoe products. These accessory products typically have a gross margin three times as high as the apparel products themselves, while the apparel items can have 60 percent to 90 percent margins on their own.

There are also category killers in the apparel industry, just like in the pet food (e.g., PetSmart) and hardware (e.g., Home Depot and Lowe's) worlds. In apparel, these stores are typically purely seasonally driven, specializing in bathing suits in the summer, coats in the winter, and specialty outfits like prom dresses in the spring. They rely on extremely high-volume merchandise turnover rates. These types of stores are becoming more prevalent as they can exist with less retail space and can easily be placed in strip malls. Apparel category killers include Dress Barn, DOTS, and Victoria's Secret, on the higher end.

Mass merchandisers rely heavily on the margins from their apparel merchandise to carry their profitability on the lower-margin products. Mass stores tend to sell thousands of individual packs of paper towels at a 2 to 3 percent margin, while selling bulk quantities of jeans for a 50 to 60 percent markup. These retailers have to continually balance the mix of sales by depending heavily on the stock-keeping unit (SKU) and basket-level data analytics. By increasing the presence of apparel in their advertising circulars, retailers can artificially adjust some of the demand for these products. The danger lies in selling too much of the apparel at a reduced margin, while continuing to sell the huge quantities of lower-margin items at 2 percent. The impact to the balance sheet can be damaging if the pre-analytics did not project the correct outcome.

RETAILER BUILDING AND LOCATION, LOCATION, LOCATION

An important piece of information to be aware of is the number of entrances a particular retail store has. This can depend on the location of the store (that is, standalone, strip mall, or primary mall). Whether the store is an anchor store is also important. In a typical four-cornered mall, the primary draw stores are located at each corner; these are known as the anchor stores. In the United States, a typical anchor store would be JCPenney, Dillard's, or Macy's, stores whose names would be used to draw more customers into the mall property. Tommy Hilfiger has launched two new anchor stores, the first in Paris and now one in London, both over 500 square meters. These stores will have multiple entrance points, which can garner the stores a big win by using the multiple entrances (and increased traffic) to sell impulse merchandise.

Other types of stores are typically located in strip malls, such as Kohl's, Fashion Bug, and Dress Barn. Lands' End and Ralph Lauren are the new men's shops, and are frequently located in larger malls.

Once a new classification, casual apparel specialty retailers are now the norm: Abercrombie & Fitch, Eddie Bauer, L.L. Bean, and Aeropostale are a few examples. These stores are heavily branded, and are destinations for the younger shoppers. These are located in larger malls, where the foot traffic is higher. Interestingly, these new casual type stores have a heavy presence in the Internet retailing environment.

WHO IS MY CUSTOMER? SIZE UP THE OPPORTUNITY AND SHOW ME THE MONEY!

Retailers around the world are now designing new and improved branding to attract a very specific target market. Each new generation has more expendable income than the previous one, thus more specialized youth market shops are popping up.

The youth markets drive the apparel business heavily, so understanding your key consumer is critical. Knowing your trade areas and available market share is also a necessity.

U.S. Statistics

- *Baby Boomers:* Born between 1946 and 1964 (over 77 million, making up almost 27 percent of the total U.S. base). This group has an estimated spend potential of $2 trillion annually.
- *Generation X:* Born between 1961 and 1981. This group will spend $125 billion annually.

- *Generation Y:* Born between 1977 and 2003 (the exact range is frequently debated, with some using 1982 to 2000 instead) with an estimated size of up to 76 million. This group has an estimated spend potential of more than $70 billion annually.

- *Internet generation (sometimes called Generation Z):* Born after 1991. I have no statistics on this group other than that they are expected to be the fastest growing and most technologically advanced group, and to have the highest spend potential of any group. They are more aware of trends and celebrity fashions and will change their style in an afternoon. They have no comparison to life from before the Internet, MySpace, YouTube, Twitter, or Google. Social media is a way of life, not a nice-to-have.

- *Innovators:* After 2000. This group will have no bounds of restrictions, and will develop new sciences that we cannot even imagine today. Their spend potential cannot even be estimated today, as there is no comparison to any other group or generation beforehand.

EVOLUTION OF A BRAND: NOT YOUR FATHER'S BLUE JEANS

A perfect example of a brand that has been able to adapt to the changing times and consumer preferences is Levi's. They were once known as the workingman's jeans, but you can now go into a Levi's store and get a complete outfit, including socks, jeans, belts, shirts, jackets, skirts, slacks, and coats—even purses and watches. There are more than 50 brands of blue jeans, which is a misnomer since "blue" jeans now come in any color you want.

Premium, or designer, jeans can cost between $500 and $950 a pair. These high-end products are not for all consumers, and knowing which ones to target is a science. Being able to utilize all available data is not only a necessity, but is critical to today's business environment. The marketing research firm NPD specializes in the collection of apparel and electronics data. This can be used to help you evaluate merchandise trends both inside and outside of your retail channel. Other companies such as Spectra Marketing collaborate with NPD,

ACNielsen, MRI, and others to build a trade area share perspective of the Standard Industrial Classification (SIC). This unique perspective can provide insight into how much money is available to be spent on a merchandise class, versus how much merchandise is available. Is there a saturation of merchandise and not enough buying power? It is a rough share of retail trade.

DIVERSIFICATION: SPREAD RISKS OVER MULTIPLE BUSINESSES

By diversifying into multiple types of apparel merchandise groups, retailers can significantly reduce exposure and risk while at the same time taking full advantage of the fast-paced fashion styles and trends. Companies such as the British-based Arcadia Group do this very well, with Arcadia encompassing eight separate clothing brands. They have developed a well-thought-out strategy with both high-end and basic brands as well as highly seasonal on-trend brands. This diversification allows retailers like Arcadia to minimize their risks in following the fashion industry's lead on new hot styles. The risk is not eliminated, though, and the analytics is still a considerable component in forecasting and modeling. One tactic that is commonly followed is to use the sales of the fashion-leading brands as a barometer of trends to come. These trend-setting designs of yesterday are typically the designs found in the basics categories today, at a reduced price (mass merchandised). Maintaining the correct mix of retail brands, as well as the mix of merchandise across all the brands, is very important.

Another tactic is to be geographically diversified. H&M (Hennes & Mauritz), a Swedish clothing company, does this very well. Known to be a discount fashion retailer with the slogan "Fashion and quality at the best prices," H&M is now in 24 countries with more than 1,300 stores. Recent news briefings say H&M is ready to expand into the Tempe, Arizona, market with multiple store openings. (This market is frequently used by foreign stores as a testing ground to break into the United States; U.K. store Tesco also opened stores in this market recently.) This diversification allows the company to monitor trends (buying patterns) within its own stores to gauge the changing marketplace. This can work across different countries and even across regions, especially with seasonal changes, as these can occur quickly. Again, this type of analysis is data intensive, is complex, and requires constant evaluation. Both merchandise mix and seasonality measurements are essential to success. Knowing that styles can be launched in one part of the world and then blended into your mix across the globe as they catch on can be very financially rewarding.

H&M is also leading the industry in lead-time and logistics. Lead time is often referred to as just-in-time (JIT) ordering and involves getting product to the store just before you run out. Logistics is managing the process of getting the merchandise from point A to point B, similar to getting it from the warehouse to the store in the shortest amount of time possible. Having the data to manage these complex relationships is crucial, and big or small, all apparel companies need to do this accurately.

CRITICAL, NEED-TO-KNOW INFORMATION IN APPAREL ANALYTICS

There are many factors to consider when delving into apparel analytics. One of the most difficult to control for is seasonality and seasonal geographies. Most retailers plan their apparel mix of merchandise up to 14 months in advance, and many retailers place orders from overseas (e.g., China and Central Asia). Once these orders are placed, it is nearly impossible to change the ship-to-receive dates, so this merchandise is arriving whether you are ready and prepared for it or not. Since the majority of apparel merchandise is based on seasons, having an unusually long winter can be disastrous, as you will shortly be receiving the spring merchandise. This is when analytics can play a really big part, by helping to identify which extra merchandise can be marked down without taking a dramatic loss. The next sections go into the seasonality factors and provide case studies of how to work around some hurdles.

Seasonality: Styles Change like the Wind

Unlike general merchandise, apparel merchandising is held strictly to a season. Once a season (spring, summer, fall, or winter) is nearing an end, the merchandise associated with that season is put through a steep markdown process. Usually the first markdown is 50 percent, and then it quickly nears 75 percent off. Once this level is hit the remaining stock is removed from the store and sent to clearance stores for sale. This markdown process can be extremely costly and heavily reduces margin on any remaining stock. If the initial purchase forecast was off even slightly, the consequences will be felt.

A season can also focus on an event such as a prom, Easter, Christmas, or sporting events (for example, the Melbourne Cup in Australia), to name a few. These events can last as few as one or two days, but can generate huge sales volumes. If the retailer is not prepared for these special dates, the loss can be extreme. All apparel merchants run by a seasonal calendar. They also use a geographical seasonal map. The calendar just shows the seasonal dates to help judge the days before a seasonal change. The map shows each geographical season zone as a band across the country, referred to as a merchandise zone. In the United States, these zones start in the Deep South (Florida through Alabama) and end in Southern California. There are generally six bands of seasons that compose the merchandise zones. Mass merchants and larger apparel chains are the ones that make the most use of zone maps.

Australia has its own seasonal zone map, although it is exactly opposite that of the United States, with the colder climate zones across the southern regions. In any case, most chains (retailers with multiple stores across a geography) will apply a geographical seasonal zone map to their strategy.

Most distribution centers are located within these merchandise zones and will stock the merchandise from their specified zones. The merchandise distribution will follow these zones closely. For example, the stores in Florida will receive the spring fashions sooner than the stores in the Midwest. The Southern stores will also receive a larger allotment of the goods that trade better in a warmer climate. The distribution of goods is another example of a perfect use of data. By setting the demand curve based on seasonality, the stores will receive their assortment just in time.

The analytics can be an essential tool in calculating the sales volume (demand curve) before the product is purchased as well as the forecasted markdown and pricing tiers. Demand curves are heavily dependent on the seasonality factor. If a price is reduced (slightly) early on, while demand is still high, the margins can be saved with less merchandise being sent through the markdown process. The use of demand curves is as much art as science when done correctly, but either way the data is an essential part of the process.

As you can see, data-driven (fact-based) decisions are key where apparel is concerned. Understanding the previous year's trends as well as the current season's trends is critical to making the correct decisions. Knowing quickly what products are selling with others can affect your daily price reductions, which dramatically impact margins. This level of analytics is not for the weak of heart. When you consider that most apparel buyers are making decisions on what they will carry (colors, styles, lengths, and patterns) and how much they will buy 12 months in advance, one small mistake can be costly and affect your whole seasonal financial outcome.

Seasonal Counterpoint

Although the majority of apparel products will follow the seasonal calendar, there are some categories that sell evenly across all months. Packaged apparel (for example, underwear, sports socks, T-shirts, hosiery) is known as the commodity products of the apparel world, and many retailers will carry a broad assortment of these nonseasonal products all year to maintain some set level of income. Some retail brands are designed specifically to avoid the ups and downs of seasons. A good example is Limited Brands, with their flagship brand Victoria's Secret. There is very little, if any, seasonable change to their marketing, and their sales continue to climb. Their expected sales are more than $7 billion (an 11 percent comparable store increase was expected for the third quarter of 2010), and have been the driving force behind Limited Brands' success.

Merchandise Placement and Presentation: From Racks to Riches

Store personnel will always place the newest and freshest styles up front in the main aisle, usually in multitier racks (for what is called the waterfall effect), keeping the merchandise fronted (that is, facing the aisle). After a week or so, the merchandise is moved to spinner racks (those round racks that you can stand in front of and move the merchandise around).

The tier racks are for prime-margin products, and you will find that most mannequins and product displays will feature the merchandise from these racks.

Along the walls of the store and in the front window displays, the merchant will show off combinations of different products, and in many cases will include accessories (for example, scarves, purses, belts, bracelets, and shoes). These accessories can make three times the normal apparel product margin, and will be displayed in as many places as possible throughout the store, especially around the register to spur impulse buying. Many retailers will now group a complete outfit together while on display. This will help show what the combination will look like and persuade the buyer to purchase the complete package. This is a great presentation technique, but requires more display space.

Accessories

As just mentioned, accessories are high-margin cross-sell items. In many cases, sales associates are rewarded a commission for selling these items. Understanding the early indicators of how consumers are cross-buying the accessories and apparel products can be a huge moneymaker. This can be accomplished (on a chain level) only through the use of market basket data. Spotting trends or early indicators of trends in the apparel business is crucial and, if managed effectively, can reduce markdowns and price reductions.

Next Best Offers

A great tool that I have successfully begun initiating across all the countries is the next best offer. The next best offer, when used properly, will allow you to present to a consumer the product that they will be most likely to want next. There are systems that can generate these and they are sometimes called offer engines, but that term does not really give the correct description. This type of mechanism is frequently used in the credit card industry, where consumers may spend and pay down on their accounts on a regular basis. When we see this pattern occurring, we may offer a new temporary credit line increase, or an offer for a reduced annual percentage rate of interest. We can use extensive models to identify which offer may trigger an additional or more expanded use of the credit card. Next-best-offer applications are also found in the insurance-related businesses. When a consumer calls to speak to a representative, the operator has a predefined list of next best offers (other products) to select from, including home insurance, life insurance, flood, hazard, and so on. Depending on what policies you currently hold in comparison to other customers who look like you on paper, you would receive offers for products that those comparable customers already bought.

My analytics team developed a slightly different modeling technique in the retail environment. We looked through hundreds of millions of rows of market basket data per retailer to determine what the purchase cycle was for specific departments. For this chapter, I discuss the apparel next-best-offer model. We identified that consumers buying ladies' apparel, specifically fashion jeans, would also purchase jewelry, but at a different point in time. Most often, one week after the jeans were purchased, they would buy the jewelry. What we could not tell was whether those consumers who did not come back and buy jewelry from our retailer bought it elsewhere.

We were able to implement next-best-offer systems in a few apparel locations as a test. We successfully developed a prediction method to determine the likelihood that when a consumer purchased certain apparel items, she would (within a short duration of time, typically within a week) purchase jewelry. Since apparel has a fairly high margin and jewelry can deliver a more than 200 percent margin, these combinations were very appealing.

A few retailers with loyalty cards were able to immediately send out an offer for jewelry to the specific consumers who had just purchased the apparel. Other retailers had private label credit cards, which allowed them to collect information at the consumer level, and with help from the credit partners we were able to communicate to these consumers quickly.

For the retailers without a loyalty management facility, we were able to bundle some of the products together. The downside of the bundling was that it reduced the overall spend threshold attained. When consumers came back into the shop, they tended to spend more than if they purchased both items in a single trip.

If you do not follow up with the consumers, you run the risk that they will buy the secondary products from your competitor.

Promotions: Lifeblood of the Apparel Business

Events like sales, advertising, and promotions should not be confused with markdowns. In the mass merchandise apparel world, which we are examining, the use of promotions is a requirement. Many retailers will include some apparel product(s) on the front page of their catalogues (or circulars, or weekly ads) every week to ensure some items with a decent margin will be included in the baskets. At a minimum, a portion of the catalogue (either in the middle or near the end) will be set aside for clothing items.

Many retail outlets will immediately, on receipt of the merchandise, display sale signs on their racks and front windows. This is to get your attention and get you into the store. Many times, the margins are high enough that the retailer can take a percentage off and still make a great profit.

RETAIL IN GENERAL: IMPULSE BUYING

I have touched on the importance of product placement to increase your chances of building bigger baskets through impulse buying. This concept holds true across all types of retail, and is managed by shelf- and space-management insights. Shelf and space management is critical in the merchandising process, as it can mean the difference between profit and loss.

Special displays are used to present some impulse merchandise, such as J-hook and zip-strip aisle displays. J-hooks are used to hang merchandise on perforated boards in places where it is usually impossible to present products. Zip-strips are plastic hooks that adhere to the end caps of aisles.

Market basket data is the primary key to identifying impulse buying, and to putting the science behind the displays and locations of the merchandise you want to promote.

Wrigley Company's Lifesavers candy was a heavily targeted brand in one store I worked with. It was displayed across the store in many unusual locations, such as footwear, fashion apparel, and costume jewelry. Baskets that contained women's shoes, diapers, and women's tops all seemed to have a higher proportion of Lifesavers than the average basket. There were other occurrences of apparent impulse buying, such as lip gloss, ChapStick, and nail glue, in the same baskets. To accelerate this relationship, we used J-hooks and displayed Lifesavers and lip gloss throughout the apparel section of our stores where the affinity was strongest. The resulting increase in volume of the impulse items was tenfold.

We ran another test by adding a display of Woolite (a fabric softener for clothing) on top of a spinner rack of new tops. The volume was 10 times the normal rate.

Obtaining additional funding from the vendors to add their product to the impulse buy program is commonplace. Vendors are urged (and willing) to pay for the benefit of being promoted throughout the store in new and innovative ways.

Adding athletic socks to an end cap with zip-strips in sporting goods is an instant hit. This type of merchandising seems very logical, and it is. Using market basket data adds the necessary component to make the program a huge success.

Chapter 4 covers the importance of geography and demographics to retailing, and how you can manage the enormous amounts of data required to bring this to life. There are examples of where this level of analytics has worked tremendously, but it takes a lot of effort.

CHAPTER **4**

Importance of Geography and Demographics

C hapter 3 focused on the apparel industry and the nuanced parts that data plays in this area. In this chapter, I look at geodemographics (geography and demographics) and the role geographic information system (GIS) tools play. GIS tools can play an important part in many areas of a retailer's strategy, from site selection to direct marketing, as GIS is as much a science as it is an art. I discuss the types and volume of data required to use GIS tools to their full potential.

Since these tools use specific types of data not available to all retailers, third-party providers are often called on to assist. I highlight some of the better-known sources.

I include examples of various types and levels of GIS reporting, from spreadsheets to trade area maps. I also cover some new terminology, such as thematic layers, which are used in the best-in-class retailers. These new terms can be found in the glossary.

Not all retailers have the luxury of having GIS tools at their disposal. For this reason, I have also included various examples of how the data has been used and presented successfully with a less advanced method.

Seasonality and geography can be interpreted as being similar, as seasonality is a factor of weather, and weather is a factor of geography.

For this section, I discuss geography as it applies to a particular location, without references to seasons, specifically how retailers measure different sites' performance and capacity against other site locations and competitors.

This chapter contains more detailed and technical information, which is necessary to convey the advanced techniques many retailers are incorporating in their industries. Understanding how these data types are being used in the retail world can bring additional insight into your analytics process, especially in how information is presented back to the retailers.

UNDERSTANDING THE TOOLS AND THE DATA REQUIREMENTS

There are many tools and utilities in analytics today, the majority of which are very specific to a single type of project. Working with geography and demographics data is no different; there are a few tools designed to work with only this type of data. These tools are referred to as GIS for short. In the next few paragraphs, I go into some detail on how these tools work, and how to get the most out of them.

How Geographic Information Systems Work: Science behind the Tools

GIS tools offer a way for analysts to work with enormous amounts of data in a very logical and structured way. These decision tools are designed to work with spatial data, which is data that pertains to latitude and longitude as well as elevations and road networks. The tools are typically used to present information back to the business as thematic maps, as compared to reports or spreadsheets. These spatial data sets vary in size but are typically very large (hundreds of thousands of rows), and include information from many varied sources. GIS tools provide a way of visualizing the data you are working with.

There are many different types of mapping tools, from those found on Internet sites (used to locate the store closest to your home) to more advanced types like Google Maps and MapQuest, which can give road networks. The top GIS toolsets used globally are MapInfo and ESRI Arc GIS. General Electric, for one, has selected the tools from

ESRI, which include ArcInfo and Arc GIS, among others. ESRI is one of the most advanced GIS solutions available on a global basis. There are ranges of complexity within each product, from simple mapping to topographical layered dissections and everything in between. GIS is an advanced tool, which requires special training, especially in how to present the best map to the business. When using these tools, it is very easy to overcomplicate the maps with too much information.

GIS Layers of Information: Building a Map, Layer by Layer

There is a set process to building a map in a GIS tool, which involves developing (stacking) layers. Each layer has similar information, such as zip codes, road networks, boundary files, parks, rivers, and lakes. For example, layer 1 may have an outline of a state, layer 2 might be the zip codes in that state, layer 3 might be the roads, and finally layer 4 might be an overlay of the national parks. You may have experienced this while looking for a hotel online: The sites display maps and points that represent hotels and restaurants, as well as roads. As the layers are placed one on top of the other, the picture takes shape, with each layer representing a different level of data.

HOW GEOGRAPHY FITS INTO RETAIL: LOCATION, LOCATION, LOCATION!

In Chapter 2, I touched briefly on case studies for which precise retail locations were required. In these examples (that is, trade area modeling, real estate site selection modeling, and competitor threat analytics), the locations of the retailers' stores as well as the locations of the competitors' stores were essential. For GIS tools to function, the locations and addresses are converted into latitudes and longitudes that represent precise points on a map. Using latitudes and longitudes, it is possible to calculate exact distances between two points on a map. With some advanced software, the actual drive time can also be defined.

Retail Geography: Data and Lots of It

Before retailers can use many of the functions in GIS tools, they have to convert store addresses into mapping coordinates (latitudes and longitudes). This process is called geocoding, or batch geocoding if you are converting a large set of data. This simply means the GIS software converts addresses into geographic codes that can be read by the software. I provide a few examples of how GIS tools have been used as well as the types of data that is bought into GIS tools.

Many retailers do not have the resources to develop all the data points required to produce detailed maps, data such as road networks, competitive locations, rivers, and bridges. These points make a map more of a strategic tool, rather than just a nice graphic.

Retailers typically buy competitive location data from companies that sell retail location data, such as Nielsen Trade Dimensions. A retailer could buy data showing the locations of all of its competitor's stores, including store size and the number of employees. With this information, the retailer could produce a map of all of its stores in relation to the competitor's locations. This would be considered one layer.

Next, the retailer would buy population data, which is available in many forms from various sources. In the United States, the data is available from the Census Bureau or from companies such as GDT, which also includes new home sales (which can be handy in predicting population shifts). Other countries, such as Australia, have access to this level of population data from government census sites such as the Australian Bureau of Statistics. Most third-party sources for population data will group the data to some aggregate level such as block group, zip code, postal code, or carrier route before selling it. Population by postal code would be another layer.

There are companies such as ACNielsen and Spectra Marketing that specialize in adding more detailed data to the aggregate levels just mentioned. Among the most sought after are household income levels and competitor sales. Sales estimates for retailers in mass merchandise, supercenter, and grocery stores are critical in estimating share of wallet and market share at the mapping location. Depending on the classification of trade (SIC code), other sources of data are available, such as National Purchase Diary for apparel retailers. Each of these would be a subsequent layer.

You would also need Topologically Integrated Geographic Encoding and Referencing (TIGER) files. TIGER files are sourced from the

U.S. Census Bureau, and contain boundary outlines of all counties, cities, and states as well as road networks. A varied level of road network data (including major roads like freeways and urban neighborhood roads) is available, depending on your country or region. Again, more layers.

Each of these data sources would be considered a separate layer that would be presented on a map produced by a GIS tool. As you can see, the level of complexity is compounded with each new layer added to the map.

Retail Data: Internal Data Collection

Retailers are collecting data at differing levels of detail. Some retailers in such companies as Best Buy and Kmart ask their customers for their zip code at the POS. This data is stored on the transaction record for later analysis. Some retailers, such as Tesco, have loyalty cards that are also scanned at the point of sale (POS) and stored. Other retailers use both methods, which allows the retailer to tag every transaction, regardless of the tender type. The transactions with zip codes assigned to them can be presented on a map showing the number of transactions by zip code.

Once you add population into the equation, penetration of total transactions can be displayed in shades of gray. Another type of visualization would be to show the sales penetration from grocery products versus general merchandise and apparel (GM&A) products, by zip code.

Retailers frequently question whether their sales are driven by income levels or size of population. GIS tools can start to answer questions like this.

Retail Trade Areas: Differing Methods for Debate

Retailers use different methods when defining trade areas (spheres of influence). The primary trade area is the geography from which approximately 60 percent to 80 percent of your sales originate. There are a variety of ways to define trade areas, and they differ in their accuracy and statistical integrity. The best estimated trade areas take into account factors such as population densities, competitive locations, demographics, housing, and lifestyle characteristics, as well as physical barriers and access patterns (such as road networks). The core data behind these methods would be POS data (either zip code or loyalty consumer data), which is collected at the retailer's stores.

Alternative (but less accurate) methods are radii, which are just circles or rings drawn around a point (see Exhibit 4.1) and drive time, or county-based trade area definitions. With this method, a circle is drawn around the retailer at one-, three-, and five-mile intervals. When estimating trade areas with either the POS data method or with the less accurate radii, care needs to be taken to accurately present the conclusion. Estimating trade areas requires skilled judgment and experience.

Another method to determine a relative trade area, used heavily by grocery and supermarket chains, is called the gravity model (see Exhibit 4.2). This method, which is more accurate than a simple radii model, still has its limitations. Gravity models will typically use a centroid (the center point on the map) for the targeted location (possibly a new site) and then calculate the potential strength to draw a consumer to this site versus the strength an existing competitor site may have, using distance as the metric in the calculation (sometimes called a *distance decay curve*). Since these models are radii designs, they are inherently problematic, as they do not include barriers to trade

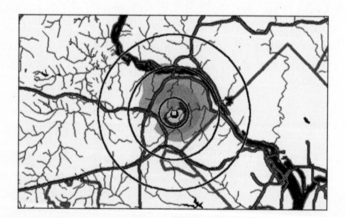

Exhibit 4.1 Radii (Radius) Method: With One-Mile, Three-Mile, and Five-Mile Rings

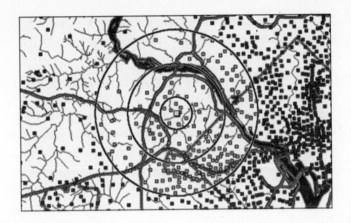

Exhibit 4.2 Gravity Model

(rivers, expressways, parks, and so on). This method is used heavily when evaluating a potential new site. The strength will determine the five-year sales estimates as well as breakeven requirements.

The most common representation of trade areas is through zip codes. A very simple style is to use the radius line (in Exhibit 4.3,

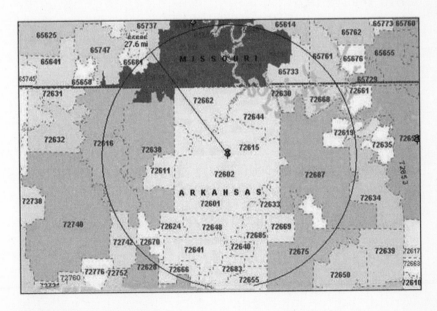

Exhibit 4.3 Zip Code Method

I use a 27-mile radius) across the zip codes around a store. You can build the spreadsheets with zip code variables once the map is drawn.

Zip Code Data: Forecasting Application Volume by Store

One of our retail partners did not have geodemographics data or GIS software, but wanted to understand where credit card applications and new accounts were coming from. They also wanted to set realistic store-level goals, which had never been set before. Lastly, they wanted to know something about their consumers' education levels, income, and home values (in aggregate). We were able to pull both the application and approved data by accounts at the zip code level.

We were able to pull basic population levels, education levels, and income and housing value data for each zip code. By following the sphere of influence (60 percent to 80 percent of total population) method of defining a trade area, we were able to draw some good conclusions (see the geodemographics report in the next section).

NOW THAT WE UNDERSTAND THE TOOL AND THE DATA, WHAT DO WE DO?

This section goes into detail on why we needed to develop this perspective and why we settled on this level, across many cases. You always have to be aware of what tools you have to work with and how to work around tool limitations. Just because you do not have specific software doesn't mean you cannot obtain meaningful insights from the available data.

Card Preference Opportunity by Zip Code: Case Study

The challenge in one case was to identify optimal credit card growth without many of the typically available data points. For each store, we needed to forecast the maximum population base that we could likely convert to a specific credit card.

No market basket data was available for this study, but we were able to use application data by zip code as a proxy. The business needed a way to better target where our opportunities for debit, credit, and private-label accounts would come from. There was also a need to identify which retail site (store) was best suited for each card product. To do this, we pulled all applications for the last 18 months and assigned them to their respective zip codes (the zip codes had been previously assigned to a store). We then pulled the geodemographics data along with census and prospect data for each zip code in the United States. At this stage we knew the number of applications (total and approved), the total number of creditworthy households (prospect database), the average household income, education levels, and many other data points including total zip code population (of residents 18 years or older). But we kept the metrics to no more than 11 at any time. We found that going over 11 data points to measure opportunities diluted the outcome.

From this study, we were able to not only identify the best stores for each product, but also the specific zip code where the best segments would come from. Again, we did not use retail data here, but kept the basic concept in place and used different data sources to keep the modeling intact. We were able to predict the card preference (credit card, private label credit card, or debit) by zip code, and reduce the marketing expenses by knowing which product to highlight.

The example in Exhibit 4.4 began with two rules:

1. Traditional stores would have a consumer pull of 10 miles.
2. Supercenter-type stores would have a consumer pull of 25 miles, as shown in column D.

We were able to calculate each zip code's distance from the store (column D), by assigning latitude and longitudes to the zip centroid (center of the zip code). The zip codes and pertinent data have been altered for this example.

The following is an explanation of each column in the Exhibit 4.4 spreadsheet:

- Column A: The store number being evaluated (home store).
- Column B: The zip code that the home store is located in.
- Column C: The zip code nearest to the home store.
- Column D: The distance each zip code is from the store. This is the column that the spreadsheet is sorted on.

Trade Area Zip Code Assignment with Geodemographic Attributes

Store Num	Home Store Zip Code	Nearest Zip Code	Distance from Store	House-hold Count	Credit Eligible House-holds	Credit Eligible HHs >425	Apps by Zip	Approved Apps by Zip	Approved %	Total Store Apps	Total Store Apps Apprv	Accum Pnttrn %	Education Levels			Avg HH Income	Per Capita Income	Avg Home Value $$
													Up to High School	Some College up to Assoc	Bach and Above			
1	12345	12345	1.47	8,472	7,497	5,248	150	47	31%	998	245	15.0%	3,948	3,565	3,073	44,149	23,052	103,200
1	12345	12346	3.11	14,292	13,216	9,251	630	136	22%	998	245	78.2%	8,103	7,002	4,313	37,435	18,215	92,500
1	12345	12347	5.66	4,622	4,510	3,157	156	35	22%	998	245	93.8%	2,399	1,789	1,091	45,910	19,403	95,200
1	12345	12348	6.02	984	1,073	751	13	4	31%	998	245	95.1%						
1	12345	12349	6.10	464	487	341	17	6	35%	998	245	96.8%	248	160	97	39,107	16,741	101,100
1	12345	12350	6.60	181	215	151	9	9	100%	998	245	97.7%	9		1	21,667	12,661	9,999
1	12345	12351	12.47	1,762	1,639	1,147	56	19	34%	998	245	103.3%	1,243	855	341	37,647	16,993	94,800
				30,777	28,637	20,046	1,031	256	25%	998	245		15,950	13,371	8,916	37,653	17,844	82,800
																Average	Average	Average
2	12356	12356	1.96	1,343	1,133	793	48	5	10%	4,467	824	1.1%						
2	12356	12357	2.95	11,929	10,150	7,105	1,924	317	16%	4,467	824	44.1%	7,189	6,485	2,593	30,503	16,577	76,900
2	12356	12358	7.77	210	188	132	23	3	13%	4,467	824	44.7%						
2	12356	12359	9.53	826	707	495	96	11	11%	4,467	824	46.8%	419	260	59	26,711	14,757	58,500
2	12356	12360	11.56	1,128	939	657	33	5	15%	4,467	824	47.5%						
2	12356	12361	12.12	1,218	1,033	723	135	18	13%	4,467	824	50.6%	849	417	143	27,177	15,131	78,800
2	12356	12362	13.67	749	610	427	94	13	14%	4,467	824	52.7%	608	279	96	29,276	13,193	65,400
2	12356	12363	13.80	367	321	225	58	13	22%	4,467	824	54.0%	320	95	52	31,923	11,766	46,200
2	12356	12364	14.67	239	207	145	23	2	9%	4,467	824	54.5%	124	77	18	22,692	14,021	56,300
2	12356	12365	15.12	561	484	339	87	23	26%	4,467	824	56.4%	346	246	92	30,217	13,652	56,400
2	12356	12366	15.39	1,038	887	621	115	26	23%	4,467	824	59.0%	593	421	132	27,679	14,864	63,100
2	12356	12367	15.65	274	229	160	28	5	18%	4,467	824	59.6%	236	82	50	25,714	13,521	54,200
2	12356	12368	18.17	206	165	116	31	5	16%	4,467	824	60.3%	136	61	31	24,231	10,942	45,000
2	12356	12369	18.32	1,207	981	687	152	33	22%	4,467	824	63.7%	800	458	291	22,467	14,680	54,200
2	12356	12370	19.49	70	62	43	11	1	9%	4,467	824	64.0%	105	37	8	28,125	11,453	55,000
2	12356	12371	22.20	156	129	90	32	2	6%	4,467	824	64.7%	54	28	12	24,000	9,751	34,200
2	12356	12372	24.44	157	121	85	9	2	22%	4,467	824	64.9%	18	13	7	32,857	14,382	60,000
2	12356	12373	27.07	292	237	166	29	4	14%	4,467	824	65.5%	129	51	15	19,779	10,045	36,700
				21,970	18,583	13,008	2,928	488	17%	4,467	824		11,926	9,010	3,599	26,890	13,249	56,060
																Average	Average	Average

Where Store 1 would be a traditional layout and 2 would be a super center

Exhibit 4.4 Geography and Demographics without GIS Tools

- Column E: The estimated household counts for each zip code from the U.S. Census Bureau.

- Column F: The number of credit-eligible households in each zip code. This data can be purchased from many sources and can be very useful in determining where your sales can come from.

- Column G: For this study, we wanted only households with credit scores greater than 425. This was the cutoff point at which we wanted to send out our higher-ticket sales brochures. This column shows the maximum number of households we would market to.

- Column H: The total actual number of credit applications we received from this zip code.

- Column I: The total number of approved applications.

- Column J: The percentage of applications that were approved.

- Column K: The total number of applications that were received from this store.

- Column L: The count of total approved applications from this store.

- Column M: The running average of approved applications. We used this column to help gauge the optimum distance to market to.

- Columns N, O, and P: These columns group households based on education levels. We wanted to determine whether education levels had any bearing on applications or approved applications.

- Column Q: Average household income for each zip code.

- Column R: Average per capita income.

- Column S: Average home value in dollars.

As you can see, there is a good blending of U.S. Census Bureau data and proprietary information. This is a good example of adding value to your database from multiple sources.

This report was used to set store-level applications goals by zip code. I was able to maximize our return on investment for the marketing dollars spent by assigning vendors to particular stores where the highest upside potential for new accounts existed. Before this method was available, we would use store sales volume as our only guide, which had its limitations. Because of this detail, we were able to distinguish between dual card (full-function credit card), always card (all-occasion card), and private-label credit card (used only with a specific retailer) forecasts. This is a perfect example of best practices.

Exhibit 4.5 is a portion from our CRM analytics plan, which was submitted as a result of the zip code report. The project plan, including store-level goals, was all based on zip code forecast models.

2005 Analytics Strategy

Acquisitions

Project: Store trade area
Goals: Assign zip codes to specific stores
Business impact: Application forecasting; vendor target stores

Business Case:
Supports plan new account and life-cycle programs:
VTEV = $NNNN
ATEV = $NNNN
CLI = $NNNN

• Develop store-level trade area model:
  Zip-code-level analysis
  Income, education, home values
  Competitor impact on acquisition levels

• Direct mail programs:
  Target specific zip codes for best results

• Identify high potential credit card geography

• Vendor store selection; Application projections

• Identify TOP potential stores for vendor assignment

ETA – Q1 2005
  - Staged rollout
  - Implement March 2005

Sales and Share Shift

Project: Department-level sales analysis
Goals: Improve share-shift by merchandise department
Business Impact: Improve signage effectiveness; increase ATV and ATF

Business Case:
Supports ongoing sales and share growth, ATV and ATF, and balance activity

• Direct mail programs:
  Target specific zip codes for best results
  Competitive targeting (target stores)

• Just Ask Analysis:
  Increase usage, improve savings and consistency in measurement

• In-store credit analysis:
  Identify merchandise departments with high percent of credit to total sales and low PLCC % of credit

• Integrate macroeconomic analysis with marketing data to provide value-add insights

ETA – Ongoing. Currently rolling out
  - Continued rollout in 2005

Exhibit 4.5 Excerpt from CRM Analytics Plan

The retailer was impressed that we could deliver a strategic plan it could participate in. By identifying the stores well ahead of time, it could guarantee adequate space was provided for a table near the front door, and determine the optimal number of associates to manage.

Example of Sales Penetration Map

Exhibit 4.6 is a good representation of a sales-penetration shading map. The tool used here is called Mosaic, and has a lot of variability to it. In Australia, we used this tool extensively for multilayered maps. The legend on the left side of the chart gives you some idea of the information presented.

The first area noted is the primary trade area, which is the heavy, dark line. This odd shape is called a polygon, and is commonly used. The dark line displays the area where the majority of the sales are

Exhibit 4.6 Australian Trade Area Thematic Map with Sales Penetration Shading Using Mosaic

coming from. Roughly 70 percent of the sales came from 30 percent of the total area.

The secondary trade area is marked with the dotted line. The secondary trade area is used to determine how far you can send out direct marketing literature and still be able to influence some consumer shopping behavior.

This map also shows the impact on the primary trade area from competition. You can see the influence the competitor is having by looking at the bottom left and bottom right of the dark line. The indentation shows how dramatically the trade area stops, which is caused by consumers in this area shopping in a different store location.

Once we completed further analysis of the impact the competitor was having on this location (competitor impact analysis), a direct marketing strategy was developed to mail special offers to convert these consumers back to our store.

MARKET OBSERVATIONS: ADDITIONAL USES OF THE GIS TOOL

Many of the best and most successful retailers that are using GIS tools today are using only 50 percent of the potential. Many concentrate their efforts on a single purpose or need, such as logistics planning (drive-time optimization for delivery trucks) or market share potential, without insight into the true capabilities. Very few companies are using the advanced functions of these tools to explore solutions to current hurdles such as year-over-year sales declines. Using trade areas at the merchandise-group (electronics, apparel, or food) level versus the total store can give you a great view of the ebbs and flows of your consumer base. You may find that the apparel trade area is shrinking in one particular neighborhood because of a new competitor opening. Whereas the total store's trade area might not reflect this, at the division level, it becomes obvious. With this knowledge, you could develop a targeted marketing strategy for this merchandise to these consumers, a very one-to-one strategy.

Another avenue worth exploring is defining trade areas based on tender type (cash, check, credit, and debit). When we were exploring the upside potential for a new credit card, we needed to understand not just the percentage of sales that came from credit, but also the percentage of credit usage by neighborhood. We wanted to know fairly precisely where to market to. We found that there were significant differences in the percentages of sales from credit versus cash, depending on the neighborhoods. Some large neighborhoods were 80 percent cash, with little potential to shift to credit, while other large neighborhoods were already credit users, so our marketing strategy was to convert them to our card.

A large building supplies company in the United States is incorporating data from Dodge reports, which is a consolidation of orders for new building supplies and new building permits, organized by census tracts (groups of neighborhoods make up a census tract). With this information, the company can produce very accurate forecasts for quantities of the products needed, based on a store-by-store demand. This forecast is being produced by leveraging the power of a GIS tool, along with a unique set of data. Imagine if you knew the average age of each surrounding neighborhood; could you accurately predict the demand from home fix-up do-it-yourself consumers?

Chapter 5 gives you a good look at the different types of marketing and how they apply to a store. It also introduces the different types of everyday low price (EDLP) merchandise pricing.

CHAPTER **5**

In-Store Marketing and Presentation

C hapter 4 was an extremely technical illustration of the GIS tool. In this chapter, I walk you through a variety of stores (figuratively). I point out different methods for promoting services as well as merchandise. There are explanations for the reasons behind the design of the store's runway, as well as the theory behind the leaf design, also known as a fishbone.

This chapter contains some early theories behind merchandise placement in a store, what the data actually shows, and how some new retailers are reacting to current environments. For example, why do you often find the eggs and milk in the farthest corner of the supermarket?

I discuss some of the different trends in pricing from everyday low price (EDLP) to tier setting.

I also discuss some of the different store types, from supercenters to traditional designs, along with the population sizes that are required to maintain a good sales volume for each design. I point out some of the inconsistent retail growth strategies for organizations such as convenience stores and hypermarts (big supercenters). I have seen vastly different strategies aimed at increasing retailer share of wallet. Some of these worked, and others did not. There are many types of in-store media, from public address (PA) announcements to floor graphics stickers to point of sale (POS) messages. I touch on many types of in-store media, as well as some success stories behind many of them.

Included are many of the specific terms that are used in the in-store environment. These terms, once understood, will be a benefit to our sales force teams in speaking with the store associates. These terms are italicized and can be found in the glossary with a more detailed explanation.

UNDERSTANDING THE DIFFERENT STORE DESIGNS

There are many different floor designs in grocery and department stores today. Many of these designs are carried over from previous years, and have nothing to do with how consumers shop. This is not just a U.S. phenomenon, as many businesses in many countries set stores up with the same traffic pattern in mind. These practices typically involve placing higher-frequency products near the back of the store, with low-margin merchandise on the perimeter and higher-margin goods near the center. There is a science to some of this, but old methods seem to prevail against science.

There have been many studies carried out, predominantly by the consumer packaged goods companies, on what shelves to put products on (high shelf versus low shelf). One inherent problem is that these packaged goods companies are responsible for only a small amount of merchandise in a store and have little say regarding what counter the product sits on, only where it sits within their small area.

All store designs are intended to alter or force a particular consumer traffic pattern within a store. The grocery store industry goes to great lengths to set predetermined traffic patterns, all with the hope of building bigger baskets.

There are some newer specialty chains that have designed destination departments within their stores (mobile phones, computers, appliances, and flat-screen televisions). These departments are heavily signed as you come into the store and guide the consumer to the area they are interested in. These stores are built on service and cross-selling, the art of selling other items related to the primary item (for example, expensive cables that go with the flat screen TV).

I go more deeply into this in the following sections.

Old Theories of Merchandise Placement

Some theories seem to live on forever. Many supermarkets even today will put eggs, milk, and most dairy products in the location farthest from the front entrance. The reasoning is simple: Make consumers walk past as much merchandise as possible so they will pick up more stuff. Although this seems logical, it is not always the case. This rule started (and was widely used) back in the 1940s and 1950s and has been used ever since. It was common back then to have single-income households, so time was not as critical and limited a resource for the shopper as it is today. In the 1950s, shopping, even for groceries, was a pleasant afternoon trip, not an exercise in time management. This was a family trip, with the kids included. The grocers would plan the design of the store knowing that the family would be spending time in each aisle.

Products that occurred most frequently on shopping lists would be placed near the back, with aisles designed to make you wander the store. Retailers didn't want shoppers to have a direct path to the items, but forced them to go down certain aisles, just to remind them of other products they may have left off their shopping lists. This method worked well, and is still being used today in many locations. The longer you stay in the store, the better the chance you will pick up those items you didn't intend to buy when you came in. These are not necessarily impulse items, but could be additional dinner side dishes, a new type of pasta, or an end-cap special promotion.

New Theories of Merchandise Placement

In the mid-1990s and early 2000s, many research firms posted studies about the ever-shrinking hour. The emphasis everywhere was on time management, with the ever-increasing trend toward dual-income families. Shopping began to be a necessity, not an enjoyable pastime. Retail organizations began to develop stores with smaller footprints, where the selection was smaller but the emphasis was on convenience. Neighborhood markets were being opened up wherever space was available. Gas stations added food to the line of goods sold along with cigarettes in their now increasing *C-channel* (convenience store) locations. These new channels were big moneymakers, taking sales and margin from grocery stores and mass merchandisers alike. Again, the new designs were based on the time pressures these new families were under, convenience was the goal, and consumers were willing to pay more for this, hence the term *time value of time*.

Mass Merchandisers Were Slow to Catch On: Does Convenience Translate into Sales?

During the mid- to late 1990s, Kmart U.S. was seeing the frequency of shopping trips decline. This was most evident in the commodity products (paper goods, salty snacks, cookies, and beverages). This drop in commodity products also affected other areas because of the cross-shopping tendencies in a mass environment. At Kmart, my division did many surveys, including in-store intercepts, competitor intercepts, and focus groups, to name a few, to try to understand what was changing in the consumer's mind. What the consumers were telling us, very consistently, was simple: "We don't have the time to shop around. We can budget our expenses easier than our time." Remember: Time is money.

We tried many types of experiments to build the frequency of trips back up, some with success and others with less than expectations. These experiments included EDLP, store in a store, department adjacencies, and convenience stores (gas stations with merchandise).

I have gone into great detail to explain each of these shopping designs in the following sections. But it is important to understand that the time pressures were not a U.S.-only phenomenon. These pressures are evident around the world. Each continent has designed its own solution, and the methods used to display merchandise have evolved to be a blend of many different retail types.

ALL ABOUT PRICING

There are many different philosophies toward pricing. Depending on the type of retailer and the merchandise you're selling, the prices can vary greatly. Grocery stores are low-margin operations and sell everyday products. Since these products are sold on a frequent basis, consumers can easily remember the last price they paid for any particular product. Department stores, on the other hand, sell merchandise on an infrequent basis, and can typically sell items at a higher markup.

The other big factor is the number of competitors in the same area. Competitors typically cut prices on products that are shopped more frequently, even in department stores. These price cuts are designed to keep the perception of low prices in place. Mass merchandisers can price items lower than most retailers can because of their low overhead costs and fast turnaround. And when you consider that a typical retailer carries around 50,000 to 60,000 different products, fast turnaround is critical.

In the sections that follow, I explain different types of pricing: EDLP, loyalty, and tiered. These are the most frequently used systems. There are many types of analytics tools out there that support pricing, and many require a lot of sales history. Again, market basket data is the driving force behind price optimization and margin management. Package quantities and replenishment are also keys to your success in setting prices.

An old saying has always rung true in merchandising: Price it right the first time, because it is difficult to justify raising prices. This is not necessarily true in all industries—just look at the price of fuel—but for the most part, consumers don't like to see prices go up.

Everyday Low Price

EDLP was a big hit in the early Walmart days, and was believed to be a big consumer draw. EDLP is a balance between advertised discounts in pricing and a low everyday price that does not fluctuate. When you set your prices at an EDLP level, you are essentially selling at the lowest price possible that still makes enough margin to turn a profit. The goal of EDLP is to instill in the consumer base the belief that they cannot get a consistently lower price anywhere else.

The ELDP model does not work for every store. In our Kmart focus groups, consumers said that time was more important to them than price, at least at Kmart. Kmart ran a weekly advertising campaign that promoted items that were temporarily reduced in price, and the consumers felt that the surprise of finding different products each week was better than the EDLP effect. Although consumers told us not to switch to EDLP, we tried many different tests anyway, with varying degrees of failure. The trouble with this strategy at Kmart was our consumers' heavy reliance on advertising. We had trained our customers to wait for the weekly advertising to do their shopping. To suddenly stop presenting commodity products in the weekly ad was disastrous.

We eventually abandoned this strategy and looked at hypermart stores to gain frequency.

Pricing Philosophies and Cost Cutting

There are many reasons to follow the EDLP path, but the predominant one is reduced cost of goods. Those retailers not engaged in EDLP universally run weekly or fortnightly advertising campaigns. These temporary price reductions cause dramatic fluctuations in the demand curve of products. These fluctuations have a ripple effect across the whole supply chain, from the raw materials to the store. The manufacturer buys raw materials based on some forecast of the demand for the finished product. If the demand fluctuates greatly, the manufacturer has to stockpile raw materials to support the wide variations. When it gets an order from a vendor for n number of finished products, it has to pass on some of the cost incurred by supporting the variable demand. The vendor now sells the product to the retailer, who in turn sells the product to a consumer. Each of these layers adds on some inherent cost, which is passed to the consumer.

Now, with EDLP, there is either very little advertising or none at all. The demand curve for the products can be very stable, making forecasting very accurate. The manufacturer can buy the raw materials on a schedule, with little need to stockpile (just-in-time shipment). Because the on-hand quantity is stable, the cost incurred is much lower. The vendor now places consistent orders for the products, and as such receives a much lower cost. The retailer receives the product at a lower cost, which in turn (theoretically) is passed to the consumer.

This philosophy has been working in the grocery and general merchandise areas for some time now.

One of the pitfalls of this process is the lack of specific marketing avenues to get your message to the consumer. Since there is so much noise hitting the consumer these days, the EDLP message can easily be lost. But with the adoption of EDLP, the retailer would have a substantially smaller advertising expense, which is a significant incentive.

Retailer Philosophies

There has been much fascination and debate surrounding EDLP. Does EDLP benefit the consumer or the retailer? Can EDLP function effectively across grocery and general merchandise? Will EDLP be accepted globally? The debate is ongoing and has received much attention recently. The U.K. retailer Tesco has recently begun phasing out their EDLP program, stating the lack of consumer acceptance as the predominant reason. Because of the tremendous consumer data Tesco has garnered over the years, stores can now successfully lower prices on specific products versus the broad brush EDLP effect. They know which products are price-sensitive (that is, elastic) and how far to reduce the price. Conversely, they also know which products not to reduce. This variability gives Tesco the ability to successfully battle such giants as ASDA by delivering value on those products most important to their consumers. Tesco, like other global retailers, is moving toward a tiered pricing method (explained next), which is working very well against its competitors.

Walmart and ASDA, as well as Carrefour, are very much supporters of the EDLP philosophy, although with varying degrees of success. Walmart in the United States has seen huge approval from the masses toward EDLP, although it still does produce a monthly circular of discounts. Most of the products presented in the circular are listed as everyday values, but there is real advertising on other products. Walmart is one of a few that have successfully been able to blend advertising into an EDLP culture. Again, the advertising is kept at a minimum.

Consumers can easily become disenchanted with a retailer that states publicly that it passes on the savings to the consumers by selling the products at the lowest possible price, then advertises them at an even lower price.

Loyalty Discount Philosophies

The process of tiered pricing was covered briefly in Chapter 2. However, since this is such an important part of retailer strategies, I cover it in more detail here. Many retailers are extremely concerned about some magazine or newspaper doing an exposé comparing the average cost of goods in their basket to the competitor next door or down the street. For this reason, many retailers look for a magic solution, from matching 100 percent of their competitor's prices on every product to devising some advertising regimen in which the prices are never stable. While matching the competitor's pricing may seem logical, it actually erodes the margin base to the point where they could go out of business. Your competitor is guaranteed to be receiving special pricing and cost incentives from the vendor or manufacturer.

In the previous case of Tesco, the organization has been able to determine through loyalty data which products are price sensitive to their most valuable consumer base. This insight is invaluable and allows Tesco to develop the exact pricing structure that will reward its consumers with savings every day on the products that are most important to them, without having to reduce the price on every single item (this strategy is sometimes referred to as *category management*). Tesco could begin offering differentiated pricing, whereby the more loyal customers are placed into a lower price group. Because these customers are spending more money with the retailer, it can afford to offer them additional discounts that the general public would not see. Many retailers have special signs hanging next to certain products showing two different prices: one for the loyalty member and a second, higher, price for the nonmember. This adds an incentive to the consumer to belong to the loyalty program. For those retailers without loyalty programs, there are pricing methods that can be employed to keep volume high on some merchandise and make higher margins on others.

Tiered Pricing

Because of the very low margins in the grocery industry, the majority of retailers today have evolved a tier philosophy to pricing. The basis for this method is to have three or four distinct groups of prices, each with a different set of products. The underlying premise is that 30 percent of your customers are creating 70 to 80 percent of your volume. These prime customers are setting your elastic boundaries. These consumers have a set of frequently purchased products, and know the boundaries of pricing between all the retailers. If the prices fall outside some set limit, they will shop elsewhere. These products are known as the Tier 1 (inelastic) items. These items have to be set at the competitor's price, if not slightly below. Typically these are brand name products that are very recognizable and purchased at a regular interval (for example, dish soap, detergents, coffee, bread, milk, diapers), just the types of products you need to maintain your average transaction frequency (ATF) and average transaction volume (ATV). This tier is sometimes called the *loyalty builders.* The use of loyalty data is not a requirement to build this tier, but market basket data is. Knowing the relationship between the products in the basket (price, brand preference, *house brand,* and quantity) is an absolute necessity.

The next tier in a three-tier environment is the moderate group, Tier 2. These items are not as sensitive to price because they are not purchased as regularly. The slight differences in pricing between you and your competitors are not recognized nearly as much as in Tier 1. These items may not be on the shopping list, but could be the impulse items that shoppers forgot to add to their lists. These items are most often not as disposable as Tier 1 items (for example, mops, brooms, glass cleaners, lightbulbs, and so on). It is still important to not be seen as gouging at this level, as these are still purchased regularly (although at a lower rate than Tier 1). In the middle tier, you will also see many house brand items (those products with the retailer name versus a branded product). This level is excellent for introducing items with slightly lower prices to the consumer, with substantial margins.

Lastly, we have Tier 3. These items are not bought at any regular interval, and may be things that are bought only on a seasonal basis (for example, roast pans, charcoal, meat thermometers, furnace filters, batteries). These are the products that actually help the retailer make up the margins on the products listed in Tier 1.

The process of setting these tiers is extremely important, and if done incorrectly, it can produce disastrous results. How many of you have seen basket-dollar comparisons on your local TV, showing the differences between Chain A's basket of goods as compared to Chain B's basket of goods, with Chain B winning?

The tiered pricing philosophy is a part of the category management process, which is widespread across the grocery and mass merchandise retailers.

TYPES AND SIZES: RETAIL STORE STRATEGIES

There are many types and sizes of retail stores today, from small neighborhood stores to huge stores over 200,000 square feet. Each design serves a specific purpose, and provides many hurdles for analytics teams. In the following sections, you will find some of these challenges and successes.

Store in a Store: Make Shopping Convenient

One test that turned into a big success occurred within our U.S. traditional Kmart store and eventually was rolled out chainwide: the pantry (store in a store). The design was simple: Identify those products bought most frequently (commodities, in this case—food, paper products, and so on) and place them conveniently together and near the front of the store. Again, through the use of market basket data, we identified those primary products as well as their affinities and designed a pantry in which these products could be found together, without having to hunt through the store. The consumer feedback was well received, and the sales increase and frequency proved the concept. We were seeing multiple shopping trips (increased frequency), which, when added up, totaled more than the previous spend per customer.

At another U.S.-based retailer, we took this concept a step further and redesigned the inside of a store from the ground up. Again, through the use of market basket data modeling, we identified those products purchased singularly (by themselves with no affinity to any other product). We also identified those product categories that were frequently purchased with other categories (high affinity–cross-sell quotient). In the end, we eliminated over 20 percent of the merchandise within the store, increased the space allotted to the highest-volume products, and placed those categories that showed the highest affinity near each other. The final design had the merchandise placed together the way consumers shopped, with more *facings* to the best products. This store had a 25 to 30 percent sales gain in the first quarter. Can you imagine eliminating 20 percent of the merchandise mix and still showing a 30 percent sales gain?

What's in a Store: Convenience Stores to Hypermart Stores

Convenience, or C-channel, stores will typically carry grab-and-go products. The types of merchandise would include tobacco, single cans of soda, personal-size bags of chips (and other salty snacks), and candy bars. Some of these C-channel stores also sell hot food, like hot dogs, which can carry an 80 percent margin. They can open a six-pack of hot dogs (40 percent margin in total) and sell each one for an 80 percent markup. People pay for convenience. These types of retail outlets are frequently set up at gas stations.

A traditional-format store would be a mass merchandiser that is selling general merchandise and apparel (GM&A), not just grocery items. These mass stores still sell the standard candy and snack foods, but tend to sell larger packages, such as bags of candy bars, rather than the singles. A typical mass merchandise store would have 50,000 to 70,000 square feet and would need a population base of 100,000 households to produce sales of $20 million to $45 million annually in the United States. There are some stores in this size that are making well more than this amount, but they are the exceptions, not the rule, and are very dependent on the population base. An increase in the number of households by 75,000 can drive up sales toward $70 million. The typical trade-area size of a traditional store format would be 10 to 12 square miles. These stores would carry approximately 16,000 different *basic stock* product stock-keeping units (SKUs) and an additional 6,000 seasonal products, depending on the time of year.

Supercenter stores are a combination of supermarkets and general merchandise. These hybrids vary widely in the breadth of products they sell. Many of the best-run chains will include fresh bakery, fresh deli, fresh fish, fresh produce, and a butcher shop. Have you noticed the bakery is always located near the front of the store, and that you can smell the fresh-baked bread throughout the store? Many stores will use fans to circulate the smell of the fresh baked goods around the store, which acts like a powerful magnet to draw consumers toward the bakery. It works *very* well.

These stores also carry a full line of grocery products as well as typical general merchandise, from cosmetics to apparel. They can run from 110,000 to 125,000 square feet, with annual sales of $80 million to $120 million. The population required to support this volume would be around 200,000 to 400,000 households, but the trade area would be in excess of 25 to 30 miles.

An interesting observation I have made in doing sales forecasts of supercenters is that the farther you go out from the store's centroid (center of the store trade area), the higher credit card sales are as a percentage of total sales. Conversely, for consumers living within two miles of the store, the percentage of credit to total sales is lowest— consumers are making more frequent single-item trips and paying with cash.

Hypermarts: When Is Big *Too* Big?

The French retailer Carrefour was the first to enter the hypermart market, with Walmart (with their Hypermart USA) and Kmart following suit. Hypermarts are extremely large retail stores that generally carry a full line of grocery products as well as general merchandise and apparel. These stores tend to have other retail specialty shops like barbers, banks, shoe repair, nail salons, hairdressers, and photo studios, to name a few. Most investment in hypermarts slowed to a standstill in the late 1990s. The idea behind the hypermart was to build a one-stop shop so that consumers did not need to go anywhere else. But covering up to 250,000 square feet (23,225 square meters), most were far too large for anyone to shop. This design ultimately made the shopping experience more painful. It was logistically impossible to shop the whole store in a single trip. If you shopped the grocery departments first, all the food products would be at the bottom of your cart. If you shopped your general merchandise first, all of the grocery products would be on top, melting on your apparel. In the United States, we found through market basket analytics that consumers would buy groceries in one trip, and possibly come back for general merchandise. I say possibly because we found account data showing up for one half of the store or the other, but rarely for both.

These stores required in excess of $120 million annually in the United States to be considered successful; most did not succeed, and were being phased out over the early 2000s. The available population to turn these sales would have been well in excess of 250,000 households. Another issue that hindered the rollout of these formats was the sheer amount of ground that was necessary, for both the store's footprint (for example, 210,000 square feet for Carrefour) and the required parking lot.

The lines are blurring today between supercenters and hypermarts, but a simple point of comparison would be size. Supercenters tend to be 100,000 to 150,000 square feet (14,000 square meters) while hypermarts would be closer to 200,000 square feet (19,000 square meters) or larger. Few of these formats still exist, although Tesco (United Kingdom) and Carrefour (Europe), to name a couple, have been successful.

Warehouse Clubs: Paying for the Privilege to Shop

Warehouse clubs began in the late 1950s and did not really hit their stride until the late 1980s. The big difference in these clubs is that you must pay a membership fee to belong, and these fees are generally annual. The merchandising concept is fairly straightforward: The retailer buys products in bulk (usually a one-time buy) at a significant discount, and passes the savings on to the consumer. Most products are industrial size, or bulk packed (such as a bundle of four boxes of cereal). This process reduces the handling cost. You will notice most clubs will have very wide aisles; this is to allow merchandise to be moved by pallet (a wooden crate that holds merchandise while being shipped) between the storeroom and the counter. Again, this no-frills way of presenting merchandise cuts down on cost. There is a saying in the warehouse business, "Stack it high and let it fly," that pretty much says it all.

There are many warehouse clubs that have either failed or have been purchased by bigger organizations. Sam's Club, a division of Walmart, purchased both Price Club and Pace in the early 1990s. Costco, which originated in the United States, has expanded into the United Kingdom with success, and is looking at Spain and South America next. Costco began with a simple premise that warehouse clubs could also sell upscale merchandise, big brands, and more expensive products.

SHOPPING BY DESIGN: TRAFFIC PATTERNS

Each store type, from traditional to hypermart, has aisles designed with a purpose. Traditional stores (standard mass merchandisers) will have what is called a *runway* (or midway) down the middle of the store. The runway will be the separation between general merchandise (snacks, kitchenware, appliances, and sporting goods) and the apparel and shoes. This design helps consumers better plan their shopping trips, as well as organize their products in the basket. This design also helps the retailers organize the departments, placing those departments that are purchased most frequently together (high affinity) close to each other. Exhibit 5.1 shows a traditional store design and one that you see most often.

The main aisle down the center of the store is often called either the runway or the midway, and is often used to promote merchandise that is being advertised or on promotion. This is the area with the most traffic, and it is supposed to produce the highest volume in sales (and thus is very expensive real estate). Many newer stores will have multiple midways running from the front of the store toward the back, and larger secondary aisles going from right to left near the middle of the store. This serves as a main interchange and helps to separate the store into blocks.

The outside ring, or perimeter, will have those products that require odd-spaced shelving or are larger in size (for example, patio furniture).

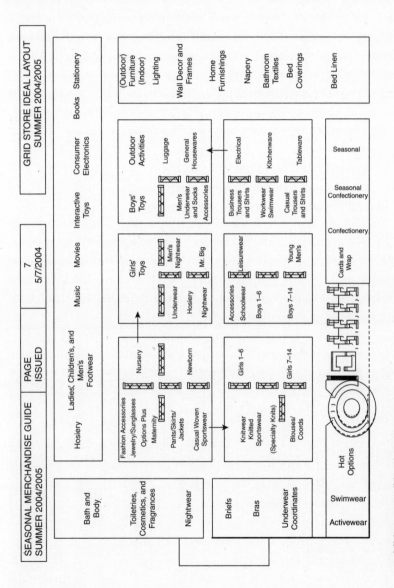

Exhibit 5.1 Traditional Store Layout

Supercenters will have a similar design, in which the grocery products are typically on one side of the store, separated by a runway aisle from the general merchandise section. Some retailers will blend in grocery-related products from general merchandise near the grocery sections. Dish soaps, laundry detergents, and cooking utensils are an excellent group of merchandise to pull consumers into the area from grocery. The soup aisle frequently, but not always, leads into the bowls and utensils section of housewares. This is not done by accident; there are big sales gains when these natural affinity categories are placed in proximity.

Some stores are experimenting with a *leaf* design, which is also referred to as *fishbone*, in their aisles (see Exhibits 5.2 and 5.3). There is still a center midway, but the aisles run off at a 45-degree angle, not directly off. The look is very distinctive (shaped like the veins of a leaf), as the aisles are at a 45-degree angle from the main aisle. This design has not caught on in the United States yet, but is big in Latin America, especially Argentina. There are many more designs other than the ones I have pointed out. The next time you are in a store, check the type of floor plan design.

Exhibit 5.2 Fishbone (Leaf) Design

Exhibit 5.3 Fishbone (Leaf) Design Floor Layout

Category Management: Science behind the Merchandise Mix

Category management (CM) has been adopted by all of the major supermarket and grocery chains worldwide. Though the premise is simple, the techniques that make up the science are very complex and data intensive.

CM was first designed to provide vendors and manufacturers with product movement and consumer attitudinal data that many retailers were unable (or unwilling) to provide. For example, ACNielsen developed a very robust predictive modeling technique that was included in the manufacturer versions of its CM tools. Companies such as PepsiCo took this a step further and added some significant proprietary analytics to the method.

Along the way, supermarkets, grocery chains, and food distributors (all retailers of predominantly consumable goods) were anxious to participate in this revolutionary way of merchandising. Since ACNielsen was the leader in this technology, and also had the most manufacturers participating, it was the obvious choice. Many mass merchandise (noncommodity food) retailers were also anxious to participate, but since the vast majority of manufacturers in the program were from the consumer side of the business and supported the program with their data, there wasn't much chance to make the technology available for nonfood or nonconsumables businesses.

Keep in mind that only commodity and consumables manufacturers were involved in the beginning, and since they were funding the development of CM, there was a lack of nonfood GM&A data.

Over time, ACNielsen developed a retail version of the category management software. The two versions (manufacturer and retail) are distinctly different in that a retail chain does not see each individual retailer's data, whereas the manufacturer does.

Categories are made up of similar merchandise (paper plates, paper towels, milk, and so on) where the type of product is the same, but the manufacturer and size may vary. These products all sell in different volumes, and to different consumers. These products are also fighting for space on the counter or shelf, so it is important to carry only the products that sell well, while maintaining a good assortment to please your consumers. Can you guess how many different types, carton shapes, container sizes, and flavors of milk there are? There are actually more than 1,000 types of milk, without even accounting for the different sizes and shapes of containers. Imagine how much space it would take to carry just one of every type. Obviously, the retailers cannot do this, so they have to rely on the management of the products to carry the best mix for their consumer.

The process involves a continuous monitoring of the products being carried against the products being sold by others (outside your mix). Also important is the ability to keep all the prices in the category in some logical order. You can't have a significant price difference within your category. For example, if the average price of a product within a category is $8.00, you would not want a low price of $1.00 and a high price of $25.00, especially if you are talking about detergents or shampoo.

As the retail buyer reviews each new product that is presented, he will need to compare its potential volume and targeted consumer against those of an existing product. In theory, a currently stocked SKU must be eliminated to make room for the new product. Remember, there is only so much room on the counter or shelf for this category.

There are different classifications of trade that food retailers fit into. Mass merchandisers, supermarkets, grocery stores, and supercenters are a few. Each of these types of retailers has its own classification system that stores are grouped into, so that when they buy data (sales or forecast) they receive only their relevant information.

Advanced retailers will use market basket data in their category management processes to help them understand the affinities between products. They do not want to eliminate a product that has a strong affinity to another product, which produces significant sales.

Many retailers are now selling their SKU data to companies such as ACNielsen, which pays a fee for POS and market basket–level data. ACNielsen in turn aggregates the data and resells it to other companies.

One notable company, Walmart, has stopped selling data in the past five years. They stopped participating in the data selling because they felt that their business was so significantly larger than anyone else's that it was easy for other retailers to calculate Walmart's share of every category (which was the case).

There are additional vendors now participating in the CM space, although they do not compete with one another. Whereas ACNielsen operates in the consumer goods commodity products, other firms, such as the NPD group, specialize in the apparel and electronics space.

Merchandise Placement: Strategy behind the Placement

When walking down an aisle, have you ever wondered why certain products are right at eye level, others are on the top shelf, and some are located on the bottom shelf?

There are many studies that try to establish the best location to place a product. Some say eye level is the best, while others say that the ideal level is even with the top of the shopping cart. Well, many retailers do not leave product placement to chance. They use advanced tools called shelf and space management systems.

These systems use extensive amounts of data from product dimensions, shelf sizing, package quantity sizes, and most importantly, market basket volume. The products most often reviewed for this type of analysis are found in the commodity groups (for example, detergents, edible goods, and other fast-selling products).

There are many different versions of this software, but two of the better-known suppliers are ACNielsen, with their SpaceMan system, and JDA, with Intactix. These products can also predict the change in product volume based on the shelf location and placement. A digital picture is taken of every product and stored on a database along with its dimensions and SKU reference number. This information is then used to produce a shelf plot plan that is in color, with appropriate size relationships (different products have different shapes). Subtle changes to product placements are made over time, and loaded into the database. This information is then used to predict the optimal placement of all products. Plot plan layouts are often developed to fit a group of similar (sister) stores. These stores are considered similar based on consumer shopping behavior and demographics, but most importantly, the stores have to be similar in size.

For even more advanced analytics, IBM provides a tool called a data-blade, which can, with the right data input, break the sales down by product colors. When a color picture is input, the software can recognize colors and reference this data against other items and products to identify trends.

In the mid-1990s, we designed a test, building an artificial intelligence logic base, which joined IBM's DB2 database and data-blades (blades are used to enhance location-based analytics). Our goal was to develop the rules required to predict the best product location for a range of promotions. We mapped out each page of a weekly circular, and created a numeric code as a reference. We then included the product specifications (size, shape, weight, and color). We also included the original price and the reduced price.

Once this data mart (small database) was completed, we pulled every combination of associated market baskets to determine the strongest affinity matches. The real value came once we integrated the time-series data (sales over time, such as days or weeks). The system began to learn from the time-series data (the frequency at which the patterns were replicated) to eliminate the occurrences that happened by chance.

This test went on for a period of six months, and was very successful. The prediction accuracy rate was 80 percent, far higher than we had originally hoped for. But the project was abandoned in the end because of the processing requirements and huge data requirements. Another issue that presented itself was the buying offices' fear that we were out to replace them.

Just imagine the sales potential if you could predict what color bag of coffee would sell best when advertised in the top left quadrant of page 3 in the August circular and placed on the third shelf in the midway. That is truly putting data to work.

Both SpaceMan and Intactix software are heavily used to produce price elasticity curves, which are then used to set tiered pricing, covered earlier in this chapter.

Specialty Departments: Coffee, Breakfast, and Pizza

Many stores today have a coffee shop and small cafeteria. These are there to keep shoppers in the store, and the longer they are in the store, the more they will spend. These concessions are often seen as oases where shoppers can sit and relax; sometimes, these are social gathering places. Many stores will have cafés with sandwiches and small hot meals. This is especially important for families with children, which are the target consumers for many retailers. These cafés are popular in mass merchandisers as well as upscale department stores, for the same reason: They do not want you to leave!

Some larger-scale retailers will have license agreements with food chains such as McDonald's or Pizza Hut, which cater to a wide range of consumer tastes. These chains can be destination stops unto themselves, and can be a big draw to bring consumers to a store.

Other Specialty Departments

Another specialty department is the indoor/outdoor garden shops. Depending on the geodemographics of the store's trade area, there may not be an outdoor portion of the garden shop. These outdoor shops tend to carry larger assortments of potted plants and gardening equipment as well as many types of ready-to-plant bulbs and seeds for gardens. They carry a wide variety of power goods as well, such as lawn mowers and power clippers. Many now carry a full line of accessories to enhance your patio, such as patio blocks, fans, and trellises. The stores with this full line of assortment will typically have more homes and fewer apartments in their surrounding areas.

Indoor garden shops will carry bagged potting soil in various sizes, a variety of houseplants, and small fertilizers. These stores will have a limited supply of small pots for home use, as well as some decorator hanging baskets. The merchandise is selected to support an area around the store that is more apartment based, with fewer homes.

As you enter the music or electronics area, you will often find yourself in a bullpen. The design is intended to give you limited entry and exit choices. There are numerous reasons for this design, one being security. The products are small and relatively expensive, and can be easily hidden from sight. Another purpose is to allow a single sales associate to assist as many consumers as possible. If the employees do not have to cover as much surface area, they are more available to consumers with questions. Many retailers require shoppers to pay for these products at the bullpen registers, which can be an annoyance to some consumers.

To help avoid issues such as stolen goods and bullpens, manufacturers have been using *RFID* (radio frequency identification) devices that are coded with magnetic strips. These devices are expensive to produce and insert in products. You can find them in such items as music CDs, DVD movies, razors, and computer games.

There are multiple types of RFID tags, from passive tags that have no power and require an external source to be activated to the more advanced tags that have microbatteries built in to offer a wider use. They come in all shapes and sizes, but tend to be small.

To deactivate these devices, cashiers must swipe them over a strong demagnetizer at the POS register, which will demagnetize the RFID magnet so it does not send out a signal. If this magnet is still intact when you try to leave the store, you will hear an alarm coming from one of two tall posts on either end of the store exit. These posts are signal receivers (usually from a company called Check-Point Security) that pick up the RFID signal. Many types of retailers are using these security devices today, from high-end department stores to do-it-yourself hardware stores.

There are many other uses for RFID devices. One company in San Francisco has developed a coupon machine that is triggered by a loyalty card with an RFID stripe. The machine prints coupons based on the shopper's identity (with different coupons for different shoppers). Another innovative company has developed a process that can print off shopping lists when you enter a store based on information stored on a database and triggered by an RFID card.

Receiving Dock

An additional use for RFID that is not quite so personal is the store's back office receiving dock (where the incoming merchandise is delivered to a store). The receiving manager can now scan a box of goods with a *remote maintenance unit* that will automatically verify the contents against the invoice—all this from a small RFID tag.

The receiving dock, hidden away from consumer's eyes, is always a busy hub of activity. There are two basic forms, or classifications, of products being delivered to a store: just-in-time (JIT) products and promotional goods.

JIT products are those that go directly to the sales floor. This sounds simple on the surface, but consider that most merchandise is shipped in some form of container, and requires time to unpack, organize, and sort. The products have to be organized on a rolling cart so that they go to the sales floor in the order that they will be placed on the shelf. The majority of these products go directly to the floor. Some products are shipped in case packs too big to fit on the shelf; for these products, a slot or home has to be allocated in the stockroom. In some retail chains, you will see the excess stock on overhead shelves, which can help eliminate the stockroom. This can appear cluttered and unattractive and will not work in a department store environment, but does work in some supermarket and grocery chains in which the turnover is quite high and the available storeroom space is limited.

The second type of product is promotional or advertised goods. These products can arrive weeks before the scheduled event, and will have to be allocated to a special location in the stockroom. Sometimes, some of this merchandise is held back to fulfill rain checks for out-of-stock occasions. New merchandise is held back until the official launch dates. In some cases, this merchandise is misplaced and is not located until after the event. In these special cases, the store will have clearance sales, or just use the stock as basic replenishment.

Some of the larger grocery and supermarket chains have computerized pick machines within their distribution centers. These machines will actually receive the shipping order from a particular store, and select the merchandise to be packed onto the truck, in the opposite order of how the merchandise will be delivered to the sales floor. For example, the products that will be taken to the floor first (such as cosmetics) would be loaded onto the truck last. This process saves the store significant time and effort. It also keeps the store loading dock clear of goods that can be lost or damaged easily.

Many retailers try to get merchandise prepriced before it is received at the loading dock. This means manufacturers will have to develop a way to print the price on the product packaging as it is manufactured. This saves considerable time for store associates and can significantly help in the JIT scenario.

The majority of the house-branded products will have the price already printed on them. The difficulty in managing this occurs at the manufacturer's packing and printing facility. Consider that a single manufacturer must produce basically the same product for multiple retailers with different names and prices on the packaging for each retailer.

Stocking the Counters

Most retail chains are now open 24 hours a day, and have to be cautious about how they deliver merchandise to the sales floor. Many stores have rules that prohibit flatbeds (rolling carts that hold cases of merchandise) from the sales floor during a specific time frame. For this reason, there are specific jobs in the store: one that brings goods out to the sales floor and others that put the stock into the correct location on the counter. Remember, the merchandise coming into the store is going directly to the sales floor, but cannot be dumped all at one time. If this occurred, how would a consumer be able to get around the store? To avoid this, the floor associate will have a list of the counters that will be filled first and continue down a prearranged path.

Most stores have night crews that bring merchandise from the stockroom to the sales floor while the store traffic is at its slowest. The night crews tend to have specific areas they are responsible for, and spend their shifts stocking.

One basic rule of thumb in the store is rotating the stock. As you put new merchandise on the counter you always put the newest or freshest goods to the back of the counter. Each commodity product has an expiration date or best-if-used-by date. These dates are watched closely, and as associates stock the counters or front the aisle (bring all the products to the front of the shelf), the oldest dates are always brought to the front of the display.

IN-STORE MEDIA: ADVERTISING OR JUST DISPLAYS?

Exposure to in-store media actually begins before shoppers even enter the building. Many grocery and supermarket stores will have advertising in their front windows, in hopes of gaining your attention. These window displays will include specials of the day, most often written in chalk or some other form of erasable material.

There are many ways to promote merchandise inside the store. One method is the use of point of purchase (POP) displays, where the display can be moved to different locations around a store. Salty snacks are frequently promoted this way. The idea is simple: The boxes that the potato chips are shipped in are designed to be functional displays: The sides can be opened for access and the displays can be recycled afterward, as they are just cardboard.

Floor graphics are a relatively new type of promotion. The idea is simple: Place a sticker on the floor near the product being promoted. These types of promotions are used when a new product is being introduced and are almost 100 percent paid for by the vendor or manufacturer. They do not always advertise price reductions. The stickers are fairly large and have great color presentation. There are also high stresses put on these stickers, as you can imagine, because of all the shopping carts and foot traffic that are constantly going over them.

The adhesive must hold them down, but allow them to be peeled off by hand without leaving any residue behind. An excellent use of these stickers is to place them at the beginning of an aisle to entice customers to enter the aisle in search of this great product. These work very well.

Have you noticed those pesky little plastic sign holders (hooks) that stick out from a shelf, just below eye level? These are called wobblers (sometimes also called shelf talkers). These signs will be used to draw your attention to a daily special, temporary price reduction, or manager's special. Many of these wobblers have coupon dispensers attached to them. There are many uses for these effects, but the fixtures are not very sturdy and are almost always very temporary. Another more advanced form of this is a literal shelf talker. These are motion-activated devices that will speak to shoppers as they walk by, giving them product information or the special price of the day. These are not widely used, since they are fairly expensive and can be irritating to some consumers.

Many retailers around the world have begun to use high-tech in-store messaging. The majority of these use in-store TV, with television screens stationed at specific locations around the store playing messaging appropriate for the surrounding products. Many supermarkets today have a TV over the deli area, showing how to cook different types of meals, all available at the counter. Many front-end register areas now have TVs hanging over the register showing advertisements for many different products, in the hope that you will realize that you do indeed need a specific product. Most of these TVs are funded or sponsored by participating vendors. This type of advertising is called streaming, which means that the same message is repeated every 15 to 20 minutes. The amount of time a typical consumer would be in the general vicinity is calculated from market basket data so that the message is not likely to be heard many times. The success rate for this type of advertising is open to debate. It is extremely difficult to evaluate the effectiveness of the ads since the products in the basket can be influenced by so many factors. We attempted to look at test stores versus control stores for a quantitative analysis, and found that the weather had more influence on what was in the basket than the TVs. Of course, as long as the vendors are paying for the devices, the retailers are going to continue using them. Many department stores have streaming cooking shows displaying new cookware, which happens to be displayed near the TV and, coincidentally, is on sale.

There are many forms of subliminal messaging, from messages hidden in other messages to sounds that draw your attention. Impulse buying is the reaction merchants are trying to get with subliminal messages. In a store environment, these messages are a little more subdued than in print media. The phrase "Sale: While Supplies Last" in big bold letters can encourage customers to think the quantity is limited, so they had better buy now.

What would be the effect of setting up a display on an end cap (the end of the counter) in the midway aisle with POP displays half full? The subliminal message is that the merchandise is selling quickly, that you better buy now because few are left. If you don't buy one now, you will be left out. This method works extremely well, and is practiced by many different types of retailers. Using market basket data helps the analyst determine the best times, and the best products, to promote.

Another form of subliminal messaging comes in the form of familiar smells, such as fresh-baked bread or cooking chicken. As mentioned earlier in this chapter, these are very powerful messages, which invoke the desire to buy. There are many smaller examples of these techniques, such as offering samples of a new cookie, a new coffee, or a new cola. These are very effective in doing two things: They get consumers' attention, and they bring them down the aisle, where they otherwise may not have ventured.

End caps are used very heavily in promoting merchandise "on deal," or advertised. There is an interesting tactic I learned early in my retail career: When you are setting up an end cap for the first time (usually in the early morning), never fill it completely. The idea is to leave strategic products missing, so that instead of a perfectly square block of products stacked on top of each other, you have a display with a few visible holes. The basis for this is that consumers do not want to be the first one to pull off a product from a perfect display, but if a few are missing, someone else has presumably been there already. I actually tested this theory over many months setting up different displays and found it to be true. End caps near the back of the store will normally have the associated department's merchandise on them. Those end caps in sporting goods will have sporting goods merchandise, and the same goes for the toy, housewares, and small appliances departments. The end caps that are directly across from the front-end registers are regarded as prime real estate, and will be used to sell high volumes of merchandise (for example, paper towels, laundry detergent, cereal, and cases of Coke or Pepsi). Another prime real estate area is the end caps that face the midway. These are the most heavily trafficked areas in the store, and again must produce the highest volume in sales and *product turnover*.

Display tables are used to help promote merchandise to consumers, usually in a bundled manner. The items are displayed together (shirts and ties, hats and gloves, scarves and gloves, even fishing poles and lures). One of the two products is typically the destination item, and the second product is an add-on. Shoppers don't necessarily intend to buy it, but it makes sense to do so when the items are seen together. Another form of this would be selling a television along with all of its associated accessories (for example, cables, multiplug adapters) when the accessories have a higher margin than the television. Many stores have these tables full of "Buy any 2 videos for $10.00" or "Buy any 3 CDs for $15.00" displays, where the vendor has supplied a range of older stock at a substantial discount. During holiday seasons, these tables become even more important for promoting seasonal merchandise. You will often see watches with cufflinks and bracelets with necklaces being promoted next to each other. Another common match is perfume and cologne. How many times have you stopped by one of these tables and remembered someone you forgot to buy a gift for?

There are many areas in the store where both vendors and manufacturers rent space to promote their products and services. This high-cost rental space is sought after because of its location. As you near the store, you see advertisements of products pasted on the front window of the store. These are enticements to get your attention and bring you into the retailer.

In many countries, when you first enter a store, you often have to enter through a gate, which opens for you automatically. You still stop and wait, and look down to see a picture of a product on the gate. You next grab either a shopping cart or a carry basket. The handles on the cart will most likely display a name or picture of a product. As you place your toddler in the seat, you see the picture of a product on the bottom. As you push the cart through the store, you most likely see the picture of yet another product on the inside of the cart, facing you. Some retailers will have beacons on the cart that trigger flashing lights and shelf talkers as you walk down certain aisles.

As you enter the self-service or express lanes to pay for your goods, you see products and services displayed on the screen in front of you.

PA announcements are an excellent in-store advertising forum. The messages can be canned, or prerecorded, or they can be live, with someone explaining a special in aisle 3. However, if these messages are not performed correctly, they can be useless. How many can even remember the last product they purchased because of a message over the intercom? Many are not even intelligible.

Kmart in the United States used to run blue-light specials, by which the idea was to create immediate excitement on products we needed to sell more of. The blue light was on wheels and could be moved around the store to stop at various products along the way. The consumer never knew what would be promoted or when, and this variety created excitement. We often saw consumers follow the light around the store. PA announcements would coincide with the light. Ham and cheese deli sandwiches were a huge hit at two for $5.00. These sandwiches carried a large margin, and we sold hundreds during the day.

Receipt Messages

Retailers will still attempt to deliver messages to you after the transaction. If you look at your receipt (docket), many retailers will print a special message to keep your attention. Some will print dates of the next promotion, some will tell you how much you saved by shopping with them, and others will invite you to join a select group of loyal members. All of this is done in the hope that this retailer will stay at the top of your mind the next time you want to shop. Some retailers will include some form of survey on the back of their receipts offering you the chance to win cash once you call.

In-Store Events

There are special days within the year that merchants use to drive sales; these days are critical to selling certain merchandise. "Back to School" and "Dollar Days" are just two of the biggest. Back-to-school purchasing can include most areas of the store, from apparel to sandwich bags and sunscreen. Store associates will receive suggestions from headquarters on how to group this merchandise together (for example, in a back-to-school destination area) based on market basket data, and some stores will publish a list of the most frequently forgotten products in order to capture more sales. These preprinted lists are specific to the schools in their area.

Holidays

Holidays have become so important to retailers that pre-Christmas sales are now occurring in July and August. Some retailers are offering special incentives to put merchandise on layaway or lay-buy for up to four months, just in the hopes that you will *not* shop the competition.

Did you know that Christmas sales just in November and December can account for more than 35 percent of a retailer's total yearly revenue? In the United States, the day after Thanksgiving is called Black Friday, mainly because retailers hope to find themselves in the black (that is, making a profit) after this day.

The amount of floor space dedicated to these holidays is growing incrementally each year. There is more signage and promotional material around the store, and it has grown to a point where it is sometimes difficult to see where you are. Every available square meter is filled with some type of advertisement.

ANALYTICS: TRACKING A MOVING TARGET

The difficulty in these types of promotions (for example, floor graphics, wobblers, end caps, tables, and PA announcements) is in being able to distinguish the promotional sales from the normal rates or locations. The analyst has to be able to differentiate the normal sale from the promotional sale, which can be difficult at times. Most promotions are scheduled ahead of time, and methodically planned out with almost military precision. In the past I have performed analytics on these promotions at the hour and minute levels. Another tactic uses so-called sale-type and price-type codes. As the merchandise is rung up at the register, the sale type or price type is captured. The products promoted on a temporary price reduction (that is, promotions that last only an hour) receive a special price type that corresponds to the time of the promotion. In this case, one could do the analytics from the market basket data.

A very worthwhile but difficult exercise for one store was to predict where and when the hourly promotion should occur. There was as much science as there was art in scheduling this. Knowing the standard consumer shopping patterns, we developed promotions to coincide with where consumers would most likely be. When this was done correctly, the results were very profitable. Many retailers do not leave sales to chance, and plan as much as possible.

Collecting the promotion data is a huge undertaking, just considering the scheduling data. We maintained a database of every SKU, along with the promotional calendar date, the price reduction, and the price-type code. This amounted to more than 16 billion rows of data, and when you consider the transaction data associated with these items, it was well into the terabytes; 1 terabyte is 1,024 gigabytes, or 1,048,576 megabytes. Any way you look at it, this is a lot of data; try to imagine 50 terabytes of data.

MARKETING OUTSIDE OF THE STORE

Even when shoppers leave the store, retailers have not exhausted the opportunities to market to them. Many stores will have vending machines either just inside or outside the store. These vending machines will sell candy, soda, toys, or other small items. Many stores will also have kiddie machines that offer a ride on a mechanical horse for a dollar. The revenue that vending services generate is 90 percent profit.

Many stores now carry propane tanks, bags of ice, rental lawn mowers, and almost anything else you can think of to build additional sales.

Some stores will also have special events where they will park a large truck in front of the store and sell massive amounts of soda, paper towels, or picnic supplies just to create excitement. These are sometimes called sidewalk sales.

Chapter 6, "Store Operations and Retail Data," goes into what some call the less glamorous side of the analytics world. Labor forecasting is one of those extremely important less glamorous sides, where one mistake can cost you millions in lost revenue. I also discuss in more detail the point of sale, which is where you meet the consumer.

CHAPTER **6**

Store Operations
and Retail Data

hapter 5 took us on a tour of a store. We explored the many
different types of stores, and the population required to maintain
the sales. This chapter discusses store operations and the data
that is required to support it. I also cover some of the career path
directions that retail associates can take both in-store and at headquarters. I explore some of the information portals available in most
retail chains. Although this is offered in generalist terms, the basics
will apply across circumstances. Lastly, I take a look at retail data from
a revenue perspective.

SETTING UP THE STORE FOR SUCCESS:
STRATEGIC USES OF DATA

Labor forecasting is the process of managing the number of hours you
are going to allocate at any point in time. Most retailers have a mix
of full-time and part-time employees. And depending on the seasonality of your business, the number of hours can fluctuate greatly. Labor
hours are generally added up to some full-time equivalent (FTE) that
is easier to manage and easier to schedule.

The following sections go over some best-in-class examples of
forecasting on a global scale, as well as using point-of-sale (POS) registers to help predict future need.

Labor Forecasting

There are many ways to estimate the number of associates needed in a particular store, for a particular day of the week, right down to the hour. Many store personnel managers can easily estimate how many people will be required to run the registers at the front of the store. Given that stores are only allotted so many hours (budgeted hours) based on last year's volume, the forecasting would seem straightforward. The saying in the store is "use them or lose them." Some of the complexity comes with part-time associates who work between 10 and 25 hours per week, on specific days. When you add in the fact that many stores are open 24 hours a day and seven days a week, the scheduling of hours can become incredibly difficult. Having too many associates at the register can cost the store profit. However, at the same time many stores have rules that no more than three customers are to be in line at any time, which means more lanes have to be opened if this occurs. If you do not have enough associates to run the registers, you can disappoint customers and they could leave. One mistake either way can be costly when you are operating on small margins. The problems are only compounded during holidays or special seasons.

To help combat this, most store employees are cross-trained to be able to run the registers and assist the floor personnel to fill (front) counters when the store slows down. Many stores have installed self-checkout lanes, which allow a single employee to monitor six to eight registers.

Many retail chains have centralized their approach to store hours, and as such, will budget out the hours based on some performance criteria (that is, last year's sales and last year's hours, and so on). To do this, they have adopted a FTE labor forecasting method.

Today, there are many different versions of labor forecasting, but each of these depends on large amounts of data. In most cases, market basket data is the primary focal point. When transactions occur, the register system keeps a log of the register number, along with the time of the transaction and all of the detailed product numbers of all the merchandise.

Importance of Accurate Labor Forecasting: The Cost of Doing Business

The Walmart.com web site is a great source for information, particularly the "Fun Facts" section. It lists average full-time employee salary, total number of employees worldwide and in the United States, average hours worked per employee per week, and total global consumers served annually. The following are my estimates along with quantities from the web site.

To put the importance of labor forecasting into perspective, Walmart employed more than 1.3 million associates in the United States and more than 1.9 million worldwide in 2006. The company says the average (full-time) employee salary is just over $10 an hour, which would add up to more than $19 million per hour for all employees. The average weekly (full-time associate) works 30 hours per week; the total salary expense per week would be $570 million. Talk about eating into margins. Obviously Walmart does not have 100 percent of its workforce working 100 percent of the time. Managers employ a very sophisticated labor forecasting method. With more than 125,000 registers that could be open at any point in time across the chain, knowing the demand is critical. The typical Walmart traditional store has roughly 25 registers. A Walmart supercenter has roughly 50 registers and a Walmart neighborhood market has roughly 10 to 15 registers.

When you consider that more than 176 million consumers shop at Walmart worldwide each week (including 127 million in the United States), the importance of controlling labor hours is clear.

For most retailers, this process is typically divided up into regions and divisions in which each store is assigned a certain number of labor hours. Depending on the number of employees and the sales forecasted to the exact hour, the store is given a certain block of hours. This block is divided by the store manager and the operations manager to fill the greatest number of consumer touchpoints (that is, running a register, filling a counter, and so on). This formula is also used to set stock-filling times. Retailers want the counters stocked before the busy times of the day, and do not want to have an abundance of merchandise stacked on the floor getting in the way of shopping carts.

The data used to drive these systems comes from the POS registers. These registers run (in most cases) off an early IBM standard called the transaction log, or TLOG (which tracks market basket data). The data is organized into buckets that use the register number to set the specific pieces to develop volume estimates. Each POS register has its own system code (for example, an ID number) that can be tracked over time.

When looking at all the registers over time, it is possible to predict the volume of transactions as well as the average number of products from each transaction. Knowing these numbers can be a good way to forecast the possible upside potential of using self-checkout registers, or to determine how many registers would be optimal to set as express registers (for example, checking out shoppers with five items or fewer).

On an interesting note, a study by the National Retail Federation has found that those stores with self-service registers are showing a dramatic decrease in impulse buying. After further study, the reason was found to be the decrease in merchandising space allocated around these registers for magazines, candy, batteries, and so on. There was inadequate display space allocated in the initial designs for these registers. This will change in the foreseeable future.

For supercenters where both general merchandise and groceries are sold, determining where the registers are placed is even more important. Most supercenters will have groceries on one side of the store and general merchandise on the other, with a separate bank of registers to support each merchandise group. Consumers will generally shop one side or the other in a particular trip, and depending on the volume of traffic from each side, a certain number of registers will have to be stationed. It would not make much sense to have 100 percent of the general merchandise registers open if the majority of consumers are shopping groceries.

Correctly forecasting seasonal demands is critical. Personnel managers in the stores are always looking for seasonal help, as these times of the year are very important in the retailer's eyes. The sudden changes in consumer volume can be very extreme, and can result in long lines at the registers. Having associates that are flexible and trained in both running a register and filling shelves is an absolute must. A store's annual labor hour budget is heavily weighted toward the holiday seasons. The difficulty comes in identifying where the volume is going to come from; for example, the indoor garden shop, home electronics, or jewelry department would each have its own register. This seasonality effect can also be driven by tourist events (for example, the Super Bowl and the Olympics), which can be difficult to predict.

Consumer Differentiation at the Point of Sale Register

The point at which the consumer pays for her merchandise is said to be the most important moment of truth between the merchant and the consumer.

There are many types of register systems being used by retail chains today; the big three are NCR, IBM, and Fujitsu. Each of these companies has its own proprietary form of loyalty and offer management, which is tied heavily to the store's systems. All of these register systems are heavily dependent on historical POS data as well as the more current (daily, if possible) transactions. Loyalty systems will offer differentiated or personalized discounts to consumers. The more data they have to work with, the more powerful and targeted the marketing can be. I have tried many different types of consumer interactions or messaging at the register. Many had to do with highlighting the amount of dollars customers had saved during this trip.

By identifying the merchandise that was purchased on sale at one retailer, my analytics team was able to calculate the discount saved on each trip. We tried forecasting the future savings if the consumer shopped with us each week or month. We felt this would help keep us top-of-mind. The results showed that we did actually change the frequency of trips in about 30 percent of the consumer base, which was a big surprise.

Without a lot of fancy marketing or high-tech loyalty programs, we were able to effectively improve the business. The analytics to measure this included a lot of store-level time-series data (collected over time). We had to keep track of the overall percentage of event-related sales compared to total sales to see if we were creating a huge group of cherry-picking consumers (those consumers who select merchandise only when it's on sale or for a particular event), and we had to do this by store. There were select times of the year when the event percent did climb, but this was according to plan. Dollar days, for example, were always a huge draw.

Heating and Cooling: Centralized Thermostats

Another area in which the management of store operations is handled from corporate offices is heating and cooling. Most stores now have their thermostats set by a computer back at the corporate headquarters, which is designed to work from historical data. The current temperatures are fed into the equation, and the stores have some leeway over the thermostat, but as a general rule headquarters keeps the variance to a minimum. This change in control has saved millions of dollars in excess cost by setting the expected demand early. Many regional power companies pass on savings to those companies that can provide expected demand figures.

Intrastore Communication

Store managers keep track of their stores' sales performance through many sources of information. One of these sources is called the store back-traffic system, which is tied to the main corporate information management system. The store manager, merchandise manager, operations manager, and all of the subsequent area assistant managers will know their sales numbers for each day of the week, along with the sales required for the week and period. These numbers are referred to frequently, on a daily basis. The manager can see the current sales volume at any particular time from the back office computer, as well as narrow the information down to see each department's performance. If the sales are lagging behind the goal, the manager can intercede and do more promotions to drive more sales. These are typically called manager's specials, and can drive significant volume.

Regional and divisional managers frequently visit stores as part of a regular inspection. Part of the inspection process is to quiz the assistant managers as well as the store managers on the daily sales goal. Each store manager will carry a piece of paper with sales figures from last year for each area that they are responsible for. They are expected to know the daily sales estimate and what is needed to beat the previous period and the same period's sales from last year. Knowing how the store's sales performance compares to that of other stores in the geography is an absolute must. If similar-sized stores in the area are performing better than the one in question, that is not good. These regional managers will make recommendations on displays and price points that have been shown to produce more sales.

Another available tool that is effective is called store-to-store transfers. If one particular store is selling a product much faster than any other store, and is in need of more merchandise quickly, the other stores in an adjoining area can send their excess products to that store through the process of a store-to-store transfer. The abnormal demand is logged on the intrastore database, or just broadcasted to the other stores through back traffic. Part of the back-traffic system is used to send information from each store to a central headquarters hub that all of the stores can connect to. Alternatively, each store can receive messages from this hub on an intermittent basis, most often at night.

As this hub connects each store back to a central computer (usually located at headquarters), the communications channel is extensively used. The buying offices will occasionally change prices on merchandise. In the past, these price changes were communicated to the stores through the mail, then the system slowly evolved to use dot matrix printers located in the back office. If the prices went down, the store personnel would have to count the entire product line and reprice it at the new level. These changes were called markdowns and were accounted for in the store inventory levels. Conversely, if the prices went up, the personnel would still count the merchandise, reprice the goods, and take a markup. This was done to accurately reflect the cost of goods on hand in inventory. These counts were written down in a list book, which the associate would have to carry around. The associate would later tally up all the changes and enter them in the back office ledger.

Today, this process is much more automated. Store personnel carry portable scanners, which receive signals (messages) from the store's central computer (the administrator). The inventory levels are tied to the POS registers. As a product is sold, the stock-on-hand level is reduced. As stock is received in the receiving dock, the inventory amount is increased. The hand-held devices are used to spot check and validate counts. The associate can scan in a product code from the counter, and the device will display the expected quantity. If there are any adjustments to be made, the associate can key in the correct quantity. This information will be automatically sent to the back office.

There are some very technologically advanced retailers today that are beginning to use electronic price tags. These tags are found on the front of the shelf with the product and display the current price of the product, along with some product information. When there is a price change, either up or down, the tag automatically displays the new price. Obviously, the products do not have a price sticker on them, which sometimes causes some consumer confusion.

Both of these systems share the entire updated inventory and price levels back to the host computer located at headquarters. If a particular store is in short supply of a high-demand product, it can check the inventory levels of nearby stores to either notify the consumer of where the product can be found (if it is found in time) or ask the other store if it can transfer stock to the original store. This is only done for emergencies, as most distribution shipments will take only one or two days now.

Replenishment and POS Sales: Cause and Effect

Replenishment and demand levels are critically tied together. In the simplest of explanations, when a sale occurs at the register, it triggers an order for a new product. (The process is not quite this straightforward, but this is a simple example.) The store replenishment system will keep track of the single item sales, and when a pack quantity (typically 6, 12, or 24) is reached, the order is placed. Some retailers will base the reorder quantity on the amount of product that will fit on the shelf; others use a method called trigger figures, which is based on total quantities sold out of an available on-hand quantity. If the shelf will hold 12 of a certain product, a reorder will be triggered when the quantity reaches 8, so that there is enough product left over to maintain stock until the order gets back to the store.

Trigger figures require a tremendous amount of data, both in sales (quantities) and reorders. The replenishment cycle time is heavily dependent on seasonal flux and current demands of the product. Trying to forecast the demand curves can be difficult when trying to account for weather, ship times, trends, and availability.

IN-STORE CAREER PATH: STOCKPERSON TO STORE MANAGER

The entry-level position in a store is typically the stockperson. These employees will stock counters, bring shopping carts into the store from the parking lot, and set up signs in the store. Starting positions can be dramatically different depending on the retailer. In some retailers, the register operators are entry-level positions, but in others, only the experienced, highly qualified associates get to work on the front end. The thought is that this position is the last consumer one-to-one point, and it has to be handled properly.

As employees move up in the store organization, they will receive more responsibility, which may eventually include department managerial or checkout supervisory positions. There will be multiple department managers, one for each area, as well as two or three checkout supervisors, one to handle each shift.

An associate who shows management abilities can work her way up through many store-level management and supervisory positions. These culminate in the role of resident assistant manager (RAM), which is common across many retailers globally. These managers are salaried and will be local to a single store. Most assistant managers will go through a store program in which they are moved at certain intervals to different stores. This process is meant to help the individual gain as much merchandising and management experience as possible. After the associate has gone through three or four different store rotations she is moved up to operations manager, again for a few rotations (two to three years). The next level would be merchandise manager (second to the store manager). In this role, the associate is basically running the store under the supervision of the store manager. For larger retail chains, the store manager (if successful) will be transitioned to a larger store with more volume to manage. This could be from a traditional general merchandise store to a supercenter. This process will continue across many store types until she is promoted to divisional manager or regional director. Under this structure, the person would be responsible for many stores within a division, or many divisional managers within a region. Many of the associates at this level will eventually move into buying-office positions within the headquarters staff. Buyers tend to have significant store experience, which gives them a great understanding of how the merchandise flow process works from both the budgeting and replenishment sides.

Because of this lengthy background, the merchants have historically had a strong say within the retail organization. Whereas some positions in the headquarters office can be filled directly from a university or other academic background, there isn't any substitute for store-level experience.

Once an employee has become a buyer within a category or sub-classification of merchandise, the next step is to be constantly moved to different kinds of merchandise. Surprisingly, moving these buyers around from candy to fishing supplies, then on to linens and kitchenware gives the individual an impressive experience level to the types and ranges of merchandise. This experience is required to move up the ladder to divisional vice president or merchandise vice president. In this position, the individual has to possess a broad background, understanding how merchandise can relate to seasons and in-store presentation as well as the affinity of one category to another.

This is just a brief description of the retail chain of command, but it does illustrate the complexity of the roles.

Chapter 7 is all about building and managing loyalty programs. It provides an in-depth look at what you should do before you embark on the path of building a loyalty program. It also covers what you should hope to gain from this effort and how you can develop short-term and long-term strategies.

CHAPTER **7**

Loyalty Marketing

T he topics in this chapter relate to loyalty marketing, loyalty management, and loyalty rewards across organizations from different countries. I discuss some of the myths behind loyalty as well as some of the hard truths as to why businesses initiate loyalty programs.

I have worked on loyalty programs in one form or another across the United States, the United Kingdom, Australia, Eastern Europe, Russia, and the United Arab Emirates. The one constant across all of these countries is that loyalty programs require a huge amount of data. Another fact that is consistent is that rigorous analytics are a necessity for managing the programs smoothly.

Loyalty programs can generate vast amounts of data, which, if used correctly, can help you make profitable decisions. You need to go into loyalty programs with the correct intentions and a complete understanding of why you think you need such a program.

LOYALTY PROGRAMS

Loyalty programs can be useful ways to drive sales and build frequency. However, companies planning on launching loyalty programs need to set their expectations accordingly. Do you want to build loyalty to your brand or to your loyalty program? This may sound like an easy question because the expected answer is, obviously, to your brand. But that may not be the result you get from a loyalty program— just look inside the wallet or purse of the typical consumer and you will find seven or more loyalty cards.

I see margins and pricing being driven further down every day, and stripping away additional margins by using loyalty programs can be dangerous. Developing the right key performance indicators (KPIs) up front is critically important to your business's survival. I have been able to leverage SAS and SAS Enterprise Miner, among other software, to build strong cases for both building and not building loyalty programs. Sometimes the data and positioning are just not right.

Many companies understand that loyalty programs can be vastly important to building rich databases of consumer data, both from a contact perspective and the cross-sell (affinity) perspective. This type of data is used to better understand what consumers are purchasing together, which helps in knowing what merchandise to promote alone or alongside other products. As stated earlier, this insight can be a huge competitive advantage as long as the consumers do not just cherry-pick your discounts and rewards offers. Not all consumers are loyal to you, your brand, or the products you sell; some are only loyal to the discounts your program offers. Intense analytics can differentiate which 30 percent of your consumers are bringing in the traditional 70 percent of your profit, and equally important, which consumers are costing you margin dollars by shopping only for discounts.

Managing this margin balance is critical to your survival and is only accomplished through strong analytics. Developing loyalty segments is one of the first steps in gaining control of your program. The typical segments are loyalists at the far left, soccer moms near the middle, and cherry pickers at the far right. Analysts tend to build a grid of five equal segments to make marketing easier, as well as making it easier for the business to visualize the data. The loyalist segment consists of those consumers who are truly loyal to both your business and your program. You absolutely want more of these consumers, but as always, be aware that your competitors want them, too. The soccer moms tend to buy a good mix of merchandise but will shop specialty shops for specific brand names. Cherry pickers essentially shop you and everyone else for the lowest price, most often on sale. If you launch a program and do not control for the right mix of consumers, the cherry picker group can destroy your margin by purchasing the discount merchandise and receiving rewards on top.

There are, as usual in retail, two schools of thought as to how you reward the different segment groups. You cannot reward all consumer segments equally; those consumers contributing the most to the program should receive the most back. Some retailers believe those consumers who shop you regularly don't need the added incentive (that is, bigger rewards), since they are predisposed to shop with you anyway. These retailers design their programs to reward the middle tier with more rewards in the hope that these consumers will become loyalists. Other retailers design their rewards structures based purely on top segment contributors. The loyalists receive the highest reward possible because they contribute the most to margin. I have found this route to be the safest, as the loyalists typically represent 30 percent of the total base, but contribute roughly 65 to 75 percent of the profit. You just cannot afford for this group to leave your program. Again, the competitors also want these consumers badly. They will continually try to gain market share by targeting these consumers. I know, because these are the tactics I used to gain share for my retailer partners.

Through the use of analytics and geographic information systems in the United States and Australia, I was able to determine which part of my trade area was being negatively affected the most. When you take a closer look and find lower sales, lower transaction frequency, and smaller baskets than the remainder of a store's trade area (all based on population size per zip code), it becomes clear that you are losing share. It is also possible to estimate the upside potential of your share of the revenue available from each zip code. These calculations are important if you are to judge how much you want to spend on marketing to gain a bigger share of the market. Through price discounting, product bundling, and tailored sales, I was able to effectively increase market share, zip code by zip code. Again, through the use of analytics tools and lots of data, I was able to determine which zip codes were worth the investment, which zip codes were predominantly held by the competitor, and which marketing tactic to use. This process saved a considerable amount of money while providing a high return on the investment. But you cannot sit on your success, because the competition will immediately attempt to win back their consumers.

Businesses starting a loyalty program tend to do so because sales are beginning to lag or the frequency of transactions is starting to decline. Many retailers feel pressure from new competition or a heightened awareness of price perception by the consumer. Loyalty programs on the surface appear to be great options to fight competition while beefing up sales and transactions.

Many grocery chains run programs that offer special prices for members. For example, where a shelf price says $2.00, members can buy for $1.80. This $0.20 discount can add up when a customer shops the entire store, which is the idea that the grocer wants to convey. When you shop the entire store, you will pick up additional merchandise that is not specially priced, which helps build the margins back up. Before you build the program, you need to identify those products that have a strong affinity so that you don't discount all the products that consumers tend to buy together. That would be a disaster to your margin and your bottom line.

In my experience, everyone believes in the power of analytics to better understand what sells best when running a loyalty program using time-series data, merchandise affinity, merchandise placement, and so on. Many companies, though, fail to do adequate analytics prior to setting up the program and can't understand why the program fails to deliver or why they see a dramatic hit on the margin bottom line.

The benefits of a properly managed program are numerous, but the dangers of building the program incorrectly are enormous.

Companies with loyalty programs use the data gained from the card programs to build specific and tailored offers for specific households. As an example, at one U.S. retailer we made a mailing to roughly 15 million households. We bundled different offers and sent each bundle to a different group of households. These households received different offers because we knew that they shopped differently, for different reasons, and for different types of merchandise. No two households are exactly the same. This type of personalization is only possible when incorporating the insights gained from loyalty programs through analytics.

Developing a fully functional loyalty program is one of the most complex and difficult projects you can undertake. Many companies that I have worked with assume that you can immediately begin to grow your loyalty program with new consumers while gaining market share and trade-area size. This is generally not the case.

There is a tried-and-true rollout strategy that has worked across many industries over the years. This strategy begins with gaining share from existing consumers. Businesses do this by gaining one additional trip, one additional product per basket at a time. Most recently, Target deployed 5 percent cash back to their credit card portfolio. But that alone was not enough to grow sales; they needed to increase the shopping frequency and recency of their existing guest base. They wanted to be top-of-mind for all shopping needs, not just mass merchandise or department store goods. To do this, they added a high-volume, high-frequency department that they called P-Fresh. This new format is planned to be rolled out to more than 800 stores in 2011, and to include basic grocery products. Adding grocery products to your merchandise mix can be dangerous, as the margin is much lower on these items, but in this case the goal is to build frequency. In a down economy, having food staples and an assortment of groceries is a smart choice, as your consumers will not have to abandon your store to get good prices.

When launching these programs, it is best to market to your existing trade areas and current customers, announcing the new changes. What this strategy accomplishes is two-fold: First, your existing consumers do not have to shop elsewhere for these high-frequency products, and second, while shopping for these products, they will pick up the high-affinity goods associated with them (sometimes impulse items). This tactic helps to increase your data from high-frequency products while increasing your loyalty from your existing customers.

The process of converting your existing customer base to a more loyal, higher-frequency group can take time and should not be rushed. Target is being very selective in its marketing and strategic plans. In the near future, I can see the company beginning to market further out from its existing trade area to begin gaining share from primary competitors. I highly recommend this process over the more aggressive plan for rolling out a loyalty program as quickly and as broadly as possible.

The process Target is following is typically accomplished before you begin gaining market share. This process can take a year or two to fully develop and another year or two to begin seeing measurable results. More simplistic programs can be ramped up more quickly, but they will not deliver the higher upside potential.

There are many different types and versions of loyalty programs. Depending on whom you ask, the range of opinions can be quite extreme:

■ *Continuity programs.* The consumer needs to do something and gets a reward in return. Examples would be shopping two more times in a month instead of once, or spending $100 more than usual and receiving extra points.

■ *Coalition programs.* Groups of retailers join forces to build a larger program. These programs have high-frequency anchor shops like grocery, fuel, and pharmacy with larger department stores to build in variety.

■ *Rewards or points.* Customers accumulate points toward special deals or products. An example would be earning 1,000 points for a free toaster.

■ *Discounts.* Merchants list multiple prices on each product. The member price is discounted from the normal price.

■ *Supporting education-based programs.* Education programs are designed to provide funding back to schools through either discounts on school supplies or checks and aid directly to schools. With each transaction a shopper makes, a portion goes back to the participating school of his or her choice.

Who Is the Sponsor for the Program?

Most loyalty programs are sponsored in some fashion, internally or externally. These sponsors are the companies or organizations that help to fund or drive the program. Understanding the differences between sponsor types is important because the focuses of the different types can be very distinct:

■ *Retailer programs:* Designed to increase sales on profitable merchandise

- *Credit card programs:* Focus on increasing frequency and spend from profitable accounts
- *Vendor programs:* Predominantly used to increase sales on their brand

Remember that many loyalty programs are not designed to build retailer loyalty, but are used to collect critical data on consumer buying behavior. A negative in-store experience can affect loyalty programs immediately without your knowledge.

Questions to Answer before You Begin

Launching a loyalty program is expensive. Without a doubt it can be one of the most expensive propositions a retailer can make. Done well, it can bring in huge gains, while pleasing the consumers with one-to-one offers and savings. Done poorly, it can alienate your shoppers and drive sales down. You need to answer some basic questions before you begin contemplating a loyalty program. These are not terribly difficult questions, but ones that need to be resolved early.

- *Is your loyalty program going to be profitable?* This seems obvious, but once you include all the variables, the answers could surprise you. You need to work closely with the finance team to include all of the fixed and variable costs as well as the funds required to support the reserve financing. Reserves are those funds required to support 100 percent of the consumers redeeming their points. What will be considered profitable? If the goal is to drive more traffic, measuring profitability can be difficult. If the goal is to build a larger targetable consumer base, again, that is a great business success but one that is difficult to measure on a profitability scale. Be careful to set profit expectations to those items that can be measured effectively.
- *Will it be cost effective?* There are numerous hidden costs that need to be studied closely. The cost of maintaining communications with the consumers can be extreme. Using direct mail (one-to-one) is the essence of loyalty programs, but a method that can be very expensive. The more you deliver specialized communication, the higher the cost to develop and deliver

these messages and offers. One of the highest and most hidden costs is in collecting and storing the data that is required to support a loyalty program. Information technology (IT) and information system development (ISD) departments are not free, and often follow the bill-back model. This model forces the IT area to bill the requesting area (marketing, buying office) back the cost in hours and support plus some incremental overhead to build the loyalty program. These costs can quickly grow when you begin to store this new, rich data. Always include the IT and hardware costs up front when you are calculating a breakeven.

- *Will it be sustainable?* Deals and offers are hard to maintain. Will you need to continually run discounts and deals to keep the consumers in the program? If so, this can be a tremendous strain on margins. Can you measure the impact of these reduced margins? Can you ensure that the cross-sell of other products will occur? How long can you sustain the reduced margins until the cross-selling can make up for the reduction? How long will it take for the consumers to begin shopping you on a regular basis without the continued reduction? The answers to these questions are difficult to measure and even more difficult to forecast and predict.

- *How long can you sustain it? Will you include a cutoff date?* How long can you afford to keep the program running if it proves to be unprofitable after one year? You will need to develop an exit strategy, one that does not alienate the consumers that have adopted the program and will allow you to get out without losing too much business, both in dollars and consumer faith. This step is one of the hardest to calculate, and will require a good partnership with finance.

- *Is there an exit strategy?* What if the program does not work? How do you exit?

- *Will the consumer feel or see the benefit of participation (eventually, immediately, maybe)?*

- *How will the consumer learn of the program?* How will you communicate?

- *What is considered a win/win?*
- *How will you measure success, or when will it be a success?* Have you designed a plan to measure what success is? What will the KPIs be? Are you measuring profit, margin, or increased sales?

TOTAL PROGRAM INCENTIVE: ARE YOU LOYAL?

There are two basic varieties of retail customer loyalty:

1. Deal loyalty: Many companies develop advertising promotions with the hopes of bringing in new customers.
2. Relationship loyalty: The consumer stays with you for reasons other than just price sensitivity

Deals can be defined as any price below list (manufacturer's suggested retail price), or the everyday pricing. Retailers use this method to gain frequency of visits by many consumers, and research has shown us that these shoppers tend to pick up (impulse buy) other merchandise during their shopping trips.

The common term for deal buyers is *cherry pickers* because of their tendency to look through all the merchandise and pick out those products priced on sale. Retailers try to keep the ratio of deal sales to total sales some balance to avoid reduced margins.

At Kmart, we kept this balance in favor of the regular price. We always tracked the regular-priced merchandise that was purchased along with the deal items through market basket analytics. A great tool for delivering on the deal loyalty scenario is called Catalina marketing. Catalina runs on the point of sale (POS) register systems in retailer stores and delivers coupons or deals based on an algorithm of predefined rules. If the consumer picks up hot dogs, he might receive a coupon for ketchup for his next visit. The offers are always time sensitive to ensure the customer will make an incremental trip to redeem the coupons.

A good rule of thumb in determining what offers to present to which group of customers was determined years ago:

- Your top 5 percent of customers will bring in 25 percent of your sales.

- Your top 10 percent of customers will bring in 40 percent of your sales.

- Your top 20 percent of customers will bring in 65 percent of your sales.

- Your top 30 percent of customers will bring in 70 percent of your sales.

I always wanted to reward my best customers with something special, regardless of the region or type of store. This reward system also made the next tier up look very appealing to the consumers. Using the Catalina system made this process work more easily and allowed us to track quickly which offer was the most effective. This is a general statement, as some retail businesses will vary. But this general rule has been very accurate in many of the countries I have worked in, and I always set this as the goal.

Relationship loyalty is more difficult to build, and retailers use different methods to achieve this. One method is called featuring, and calls for the retailer to place merchandise on an end cap. The goal is to present a group of products (for example, baby products, new-mom products) in a central location that helps the consumer find products easily. Another way is through direct marketing, wherein a new product is offered to a select group of consumers first, before the general public has an opportunity to purchase it.

Another tactic you will see when businesses are launching new programs is promoting the highest-frequency products first. This may seem counterintuitive but these programs when first launched are designed to increase the trip frequency of the existing consumer. If developed correctly, this will also increase spending in the affinity departments and increase the impulse buy.

The next phase in this early start-up is to begin increasing the reach to gain market share outside of the existing consumers. This is now doable, since you have been collecting valuable spend data all year.

For loyalty programs to be both effective and 100 percent measurable, you need to ensure that the rewards are attributable to card usage only, not trip frequency or spend in general.

On one hand, this dramatically simplifies the loyalty process; you manage only one tender type. But conversely, you have a much smaller consumer base to work with, and many fewer levers to pull.

Adding up the number of items per basket or trip would be a tremendous help in developing forecast models to predict future trip velocity. This would also allow us to determine the item-price sensitivity of individual consumers. Are they utilitarian shoppers (get in–get out) or deal searchers?

The offer could differ greatly between the two.

FROM THE CONSUMER FINANCE CREDIT CARD RETAIL PERSPECTIVE

Many retailers today have their own branded credit cards. Using data from these cards can be tremendously helpful, but also adds some complexity:

- Does 30 percent of your account base generate 70 percent of your profit? If so, how do you manage these exceptions? Are these 30 percent accounts loyal consumers to your card, or are they loyal to your marketing programs?
- How do you deselect your profitable customers *and* your transactional loss customers? Can you tell how important your profitable customers are to your partner?
- Which account holders can you influence to spend more on profitable merchandise (a big win for the retailer/partner)?

Retail credit card providers do not capture 100 percent of the transactions, only the portion that are put on the retailer's card. They do not capture the transactions made on competing credit cards, cash, debit, or checks. So it is impossible for them to determine accurately what change has been made to the frequency of shopping trips. The customer can be making more trips, but using cash or some other untrackable tender. So, you could have increased trip frequency but not increased card utilization. As far as you know, there is no incremental change in behavior. Until we can track 100 percent of particular customers' shopping trips, we cannot measure the changes in frequency with extreme accuracy.

The retailer can use a standalone card that is not attached to any credit card. These standalone cards are often used in place of a dual-purpose card, where the credit card is also the loyalty card. One advantage of the dual card is that the consumer is often offered a point-plus advantage, with which the consumer can accelerate their accumulation of points.

LOYALTY SEGMENTS: DEVELOP THEM EARLY

Segments are clusters of consumers grouped based on some pre-defined measurement. Many are based on some financial performance variable: profitability, revenue, or annual visits.

From these segments, you will need to know to whom you want to market. You will also need to answer these tough questions:

- Who do you keep? (Typically 30 percent generate 70 percent of your profit.)
- Who do you let lag? (The cherry pickers/discount-seeker segments)
- Who do you let leave? (The switchers/the ones that shop you and the competitor equally)

Exhibit 7.1 demonstrates the typical decile segmentation. The equal distribution of the consumers into 10 groups is called segmenting. In this example, it is apparent that the 10 groups contribute differently from each other. In this case, you may not want to spend marketing dollars to keep the group in segment 10, while you would want to keep segment 1. Once you have this level of analytics, it is possible to heavily target segment 3 with the intent to move a portion up to segment 2.

Since you cannot market to all consumer segments, you tailor the offers based on the likelihood that the consumer will change her purchase behavior to be more profitable for you. You would not offer a big discount to a consumer who only shops you for sale items and discounted goods.

You also need to determine which segments the consumer fits into for recency, frequency, and monetary (RFM) scoring. Some offers are time-based (good for one week only); these are used to increase

Top 20%
drive 65% of sales

Decile	Annual Households	% Sales	Cum % Sales	Annual Visits	Annual Value	Market Basket	Marketing $$ per Customer
1	8,500,000	42.1%	42.1%	59.3	$ 2,269	$ 38.25	$ 80.00
2	8,500,000	23.1%	65.2%	39.3	$ 1,245	$ 31.66	$ 80.00
3	8,500,000	11.6%	76.8%	27.7	$ 625	$ 22.60	$ 80.00
4	8,500,000	7.9%	84.7%	21.3	$ 426	$ 19.96	$ 80.00
5	8,500,000	6.3%	91.0%	16.3	$ 340	$ 20.79	$ 80.00
6	8,500,000	3.4%	94.4%	12.0	$ 183	$ 15.27	$ 80.00
7	8,500,000	2.6%	97.0%	8.0	$ 140	$ 17.52	$ 80.00
8	8,500,000	1.3%	98.3%	6.0	$ 70	$ 11.68	$ 80.00
9	8,500,000	1.0%	99.3%	5.0	$ 54	$ 10.78	$ 80.00
10	8,500,000	0.7%	100.0%	4.0	$ 38		$ 80.00
Total	85,000,000	100.0%	100.0%	20.0	$ 539	$ 26.95	$ 80.00

Bottom 50% only
drive 9% of sales

Ad spend exceeds
margin on sales

Exhibit 7.1 Decile Segmentation

recency. Some offers are based on multiples (buy one and get one at half price), and used to build bigger baskets. Knowing the appropriate offer for the right segment is critical.

Do you want loyal unprofitable customers? These customers are the bottom 20 percent of your base, the ones that will shop you only for the discounts. You do not want to invest marketing dollars in these groups. Once you have the segmentation developed, it is easier to identify these groups and put the correct strategy in place to manage them appropriately. One strategy is to let the competition lose money on them.

You cannot target everyone—it is not fiscally responsible. Targeting everyone makes it impossible to show any positive response. From Exhibit 7.1, it is easy to see where the profitable consumers fit. This makes it easier to justify spending marketing dollars. You need to understand where to make the investment, and where the investment will pay you back. The annual value indicator has been a very important financial measurement for me. This simple index can immediately bring to light how much you should be spending on each segment, as this is the annual return you can expect.

Don't forget to keep track of what your best competition is doing. If you believe they are taking share away from you, you must understand what is driving their success. Simply launching a loyalty program may not be the answer.

LOYALTY AT POS: DIFFERENT STAGES AND LEVELS OF LOYALTY

There are different levels of loyalty that can be implemented at the POS. Many retailers cannot afford, or just don't want, to have a complex process built.

Many retailers apply discounts at the register, typically matching competitor prices or collecting coupons. Some programs are designed to offer some instant rebate if you spend over some threshold. We tried the spend-and-get program in a mass merchandise retailer. Spend-and-get programs are a threshold-based dollar or quantity program through which you group consumers together based on their frequency and spend thresholds. As an example, we had a group that consistently shopped once a week and spent $75 each trip. We targeted these customers with an offer to get $10 dollars back when they shopped one extra trip a month and spent $100 on that trip. In the end, the consumers did have one additional shopping trip, and spent over 35 percent more than before. This increase covered the $10 offer and more. And yes, we included the $10 as a loss in margin, but again, we calculated the breakeven before running the program.

The next phase of this approach is to build continuity programs, which send the consumer a fresh offer after the initial threshold has been met. The consumer has met the five trips in a month threshold, with an additional $100 basket. Now you can build an incentive to continue this behavior or build the next threshold offer. Depending on what you want to accomplish increasing (for example, frequency, recency, or sales), the offer and threshold can be designed. It is difficult to build in multiple offer components (frequency and sales or recency and frequency), so it is easier to stick with one tactic.

These types of programs are extremely data dependent and require a strong analytics structure. The models need to be updated frequently with fresh data. The communications to these consumers must be managed very closely, as you do not want to overrun the consumer with too much activity.

One important point to make is that communication with the consumer is essential. You will need to keep consumers very well informed about how important they are to your business, as well as how much the program (and your business) has saved them in dollars and time spent. However, it is not always easy to measure the returns from this communication. As an example, Kmart developed a program to print the savings on the customer receipt, hoping to get incremental trips and build a better customer base. This program seemed to work for a while, but in the end, we could not substantiate any incremental business from the customers.

The POS registers are by far the best delivery mechanism to get an offer of any type to the consumers (once they are in the store). Today we find the majority of retailers are just matching competitor's prices, which is probably the lowest form of loyalty marketing. As shown in Exhibit 7.2, this is basically mass discounting with no targeting. Another mass merchandise targeting approach is to target everyone at the POS—for example, each basket that has cereal would receive an offer for milk. Every basket over $100 would receive $5 off. These are easy to manage but very difficult to quantify any incremental gain.

Many agencies define loyalty marketing as the systematic management process of identifying one's best customers and using customer data and insight to create, retain, and grow profitable relationships. Best customers are those who add the most profitability to the organization. Also important are those whose characteristics suggest that they have the potential to become your best customers. One common, often referred-to metric is that 30 percent of your customers account for 70 percent of your profit. Identifying these is critical.

Exhibit 7.2 Mass Discounting

POS Today	POS Blind Offers
Mass discounting, no targeting	Mass targeting all transactions at POS
Match competition on 80 percent of goods	Each basket receives coupon(s) based on that basket's mix — $10 off $200 — Spend and get

Exhibit 7.3 Road to POS Targeted Marketing

Mass targeting with differentiated offers at POS	Targeted offers based on account number on tender
Offers are differentiated based on mix of the basket's goods — Baby goods receive baby offers — Fresh goods receive fresh offers	Historical transaction history (purchases over time) guides the offer rules — Often buys quick meals — Often buys Coke with chips — Shops once a week — Buys premium dog food

The next level of POS loyalty starts with differentiated offers, as shown in Exhibit 7.3. To initiate differentiated offers, the retailer needs to begin market basket analytics. If a basket contains baby products, the offer has to be designed to appeal to this consumer. Different organizations ran these types of offers with fairly good success, but had a difficult time managing the margin erosion.

In the end, we decided to bring in the experts, who managed the offer mechanism and worked with the vendors to reduce the cost of goods that would be discounted. Catalina managed Kmart's program for a number of years with good success, and delivered consistent results. For Kmart, this arrangement worked very well in the consumable categories but not in the general merchandise area (that is, sporting goods, apparel, hard home, and so on), which was not their area of expertise. But increasing the frequency and cross-shopping of our grocery merchandise was a significant business opportunity.

The ultimate goal of loyalty marketing is to increase shopping frequency, increase recency, and increase spend. Yes, this is the basic RFM scoring.

A significant side benefit is the ability to collect consumer-identifiable information (for example, name, address, and card number). This allows the retailer to link each basket to a unique consumer, again, allowing the retailer to make real one-to-one offer to the consumer. I have found that consumers do not like junk mail, but do appreciate receiving offers that are specific to their tastes and needs.

The next level of POS loyalty is the use of account numbers collected from previous transactions. Again, you do not know the consumer, and cannot differentiate one consumer from another. You also cannot tell how many cards a single consumer is using. I have found that most shoppers will use the same debit or credit card when shopping a particular store. With Catalina marketing, we were able to build a transaction history by tender with all of the typical merchandise product affinities. When we observed a particular product going through the scanner, we presented the shopper with a compelling coupon for her next visit. The coupons were compelling because we knew she frequently purchased quick meals, or had recently purchased maternity clothes. Having this level of insight allowed us to offer meaningful discounts on merchandise that the consumer was likely to come back to purchase from us.

Another benefit from this information was the development of a rough timeline of purchase frequency. For example, for account 12345, we knew the rough purchase frequency of the staple products like milk and bread. We were able to provide a coupon for a product a week before the next scheduled purchase. Providing a coupon one week before the consumer would need it gives him an incentive to come back to our store instead of shopping somewhere else. This process worked very well, but required very fast processing and a POS system able to integrate with Catalina.

KMART'S SCHOOL SPIRIT LOYALTY PROGRAM

The Kmart School Spirit program was developed to be a cash back–style loyalty program. In this type of program, the rewards are donated back to a preselected recipient. Our program was designed to give cash to schools, and Kmart announced plans to donate millions of dollars to K–12 schools in a school year. A couple hundred thousand dollars was raised in the program's first three weeks. Many loyalty and rewards programs provide quarterly payouts to the donee in the form of gift cards.

The only requirement for Kmart's program was that customers enroll in the program, specify the school to receive donations, and use a special School Spirit card when shopping at Kmart. With each purchase the customer made at any Kmart store, the company donated a portion of the proceeds to the customer's school of choice.

Through the School Spirit program, Kmart donated millions of dollars to schools throughout the United States, Puerto Rico, the U.S. Virgin Islands, and Guam in the 2001–2002 school year.

Our target audience was the top segment of busy, budget-conscious moms. We felt that this was the most significant group of consumers, with the most influence on what was purchased and how often the trips occurred. This information was accumulated through heavy research and many focus groups, and was tabulated through analytics. Our research was called Ktrends and was a big part of the corporate strategy development.

This program was the next extension of the POS differentiated offers.

The challenge (read: opportunity) that we were presented with was very direct: Build and launch a loyalty program in six months. We had to cut corners while keeping the program intact, which was difficult to say the least.

The first obstacle was to touch as few POS infrastructure areas as possible, which meant no new register software could be included. One area in which we were able to cut costs and accelerate the program launch was in the use of universal product code (UPC) coded cards in place of the traditional mag-stripe.

We were able to produce the cards at a fraction of the cost, and were able to scan the cards at any point of the transaction. One consumer insight we gained from research was that consumers did not like having to remember to use a loyalty card at the beginning of a transaction. With a mag-stripe program, this is required to ensure the items are tagged to the consumer's card. If the customer was late presenting the card, the transaction would have to be voided and started over.

With the new program, the card could be scanned like any other piece of merchandise at any time in the pre-tender. This gave consumers more time to remember their card, and also gave the register operator time to request the card. This single fact was a huge delighter for our consumers and cut implementation time in half.

Kmart applied heavy analytic rigor behind the program to help maintain the accelerated launch schedule. We also needed to keep senior leadership apprised of the program, since we provided the media with frequent updates. We immediately enrolled millions of households, and within the first six months after launch, we had enrolled several more millions of households (families with kids as our target). Within one year, we drove millions in incremental sales, which was a sales lift. These were all substantiated through our finance department.

AUSTRALIAN LOYALTY

When I arrived in Australia, I was unsure whether my previous retail and loyalty management experience would accurately apply. I was bringing many tried and true retail analytics methods and practices with me to Australia. I was unsure if these methods would work as is or with a little adjustment.

The first thing I observed was that the consumers shopped for grocery goods every day or two; they did not stock up, and highly favored fresh meals to prepackaged ones. The majority of the consumers bought their vegetables, meat, and deli items daily.

I quickly understood this phenomenon after my wife and I purchased our home. The pantry in our home (as was typical) was one-third the size of the one in my old American home, and the refrigerator was half the size. This left very little storage room for food. The space within the home was designed for more space, rather than for things. Space aside, Australians put a very high emphasis on freshness, much more so than I had observed in the United States.

This was a very important point for me as I developed new analytics techniques and methods. Consumers shopped, on average, more than three times as often as their U.S. counterparts. So when calculating RFM scoring, I needed to adjust my measurements.

Another big observation was the lack of grocery store parking. The majority of the stores had little, if any, parking available, and most consumers had to park down the block or in parking structures nearby. I was lucky, as my store in Melbourne had a small parking lot on the roof of the store.

Many department store malls have grocery stores within them. Some of these grocers had to be accessed from the third-floor entrance.

In the United States, there is a term, "time value of money," which is quickly being changed to "time value of time." In other countries, the shopping experience is much more important than cutting time out of your trip. It is a way of taking care of the family with fresh and healthy goods. Shopping for groceries every day is normal and actually preferred.

In the end, the methods I used in the United States worked very well in Australia, and in many other countries, after adjusting for the local customs and habits.

FLYBUYS REWARDS AND LOYALTY: AUSTRALIA

A good example of a very large loyalty program in Australia is *FlyBuys*. This is a mag-stripe card program that initially allowed consumers to collect points that could be turned in for merchandise or airline tickets.

It has been estimated that FlyBuys is the largest loyalty program in Australia, with more than 10 million cardholders in more than 5.5 million Australian households. There have been multiple studies of the loyalty programs in Australia, and FlyBuys is always ranked at or near the top.

An extensive analytics project helped the program increase the frequency by providing quarterly payouts through the Coles gift card. Coles Group consists of a licensed version of Kmart and Target as well as the grocery chain Coles and BiLo. The group also includes a number of liquor chains and a home office department store.

The program was designed to allow a consumer to receive payouts that could be redeemed at any Coles business. Coles used the program to build an extensive data-intensive consumer profiling process to better serve their consumers on a store-by-store basis.

We blended market basket data in with the loyalty data to paint a very accurate picture of each store's trade area and tied this into the merchandising planning systems. We used Mosaic, along with other utilities, to map out each store along with all the area attributes. This could not have been accomplished without the loyalty program.

The predominant partner or anchor of the program was the retailer Coles Group, which valued the program very highly. Coles Group's managing director for marketing, Coles Express, and liquor, Mick McMahon, added:

> These changes were all about making FlyBuys more relevant for its six million members. As well as rewarding customers for shopping with us, the FlyBuys program gives us the ability to capture and leverage vital data so that we can continue to develop a unique proposition across our range of store formats.

The loyalty program allowed for points accrued from purchases within any brand to be redeemed at any of the other stores. One big selling point of the program is its association with Coles Source MasterCard. The program is designed to allow the consumer to accelerate their rewards by including the co-branded credit card in their purchasing.

This is a great example of having a standalone loyalty card as well as a bundled credit loyalty card. Having the ability to accelerate rewards was very appealing to the consumer.

ADDITIONAL LOYALTY PROGRAMS

Rival retailer Woolworths launched its Everyday Rewards discount card nationally in 2009, and by August 2010, it was estimated to have collected 5.1 million cardholders, with at least half of these linked to their partner's frequent flyer program.

Another large retailer program was Myer's (an Australian department store) MYER One program. Myer at one point was a part of the Coles organization, but was spun off in the mid-2000s. At that point, it created its own loyalty program.

Australia has many different types of loyalty programs that range from banks to airlines and many retailer and pharmacy groups.

Large-scale loyalty programs from other countries include:

- *United Kingdom: Nectar.* Nectar is considered the best-in-class for coalition loyalty programs and has been able to maintain a certain level of interest from its consumer base for quite a long time. Points are normally collected at a rate of two points for every British pound spent, and the consumer can accelerate his point growth by shopping at more than one Nectar retailer. Unlike in some programs, the consumer is allowed to grow his points to help make a bigger purchase. Because there are many participant retailers in the program, the increase in loyalty is a big win.

Nectar has strong anchor stores:

- Sainsbury Supermarket, with wide distribution (maintains frequency and recency)

- Express Chemist, for prescription coverage (family and children)

- Fuel (regular trips and stable spend)

- Department stores, mass merchant stores, and more (destination stores)

- *Turkey: Garanti.* Garanti's program has all the features of Nectar's, with:

  - Established anchor brands

  - Frequent flyer program

  - Wide range of financial services

  - Bank branches (loans, assets, deposits, and ATMs)

THE RETAIL WORLD IS CHANGING

Senior members of retail organizations are becoming believers in the idea that understanding their consumers is critical for their survival. Retail analytics is one of the only real avenues available today to get these insights:

> Our focus on customers means that we serve them better by getting to know them better. For that purpose, we have expanded our customer databases. By mining the data in these databases, we can tailor our products, merchandise, services, prices and customer relations programs to our customer base with even more precision.

> —*Jose Luis Duran, chairman of Carrefour,*
> *2006 Annual Report*

The last point that needs to be reiterated is that strong loyalty programs begin with strong analytics, which require data mining.

The goals of a well-designed customer relationship program are to increase your return on investment for shareholders, which can be accomplished by increasing the return on your marketing investment and maximizing lifetime customer value. Increasing the number of times the consumer shops with you, over an extended time frame or just within a single year, is the ultimate goal.

You learn how to choose the right kind of retail loyalty program for your business through intelligent data mining and analytics. You must evaluate all of the data you are currently collecting and determine what, if any, pieces are missing before you can make the decision to launch a loyalty program. Through analytics, you can determine clear reasons for going through the loyalty process, and what a clear breakeven will look like.

Loyalty programs can be extremely expensive to manage, because you must find a profitable return on investment (ROI) to sustain them. Without this balance, you can quickly find them difficult to manage. Data usage is the ultimate key to a successful program. Gather as much as possible and make use of it as often as possible to ensure you will receive a good return. And finally, develop the KPIs early, measure them often, and frequently revisit the primary reasons for launching the program. It is easy to get enamored with the loyalty program process, so it is critical to stay on a strong strategic path.

SOCIAL MEDIA

A relatively new form of loyalty building utilizes social media. There have been many books written on this subject already, and some even discuss cases that have worked under certain circumstances. I have been working with social media in one form or another for a few years, sometimes with success (how do you measure success?) and sometimes without any tangible evidence of difference.

Social media is a difficult form of media to get any type of measurable gain from. It is very loose in its design, as are many blogs (blogs are a form of public diary in which people discuss whatever topic appeals to them). Many analytics companies state they can accurately measure ROI, but in my experience, using social media as a marketing tool is dangerous. At best, these blogs can be very useful as leading indicators of consumer sentiment.

There are many social media sites out there in cyberspace: Twitter, MySpace, YouTube, LinkedIn, Facebook, and many more. These sites are used by individuals and groups as ways to communicate on a wide scale with other people with similar interests. Sites such as Twitter allow the user to talk about anything, at any time, for any reason, 140 characters at a time. There is no moderator or central point, which can make it extremely difficult to monitor or score the conversations for relevance.

Many people I speak with believe they are using social media if they are involved in Internet search engine optimization (SEO), keyword searching (tagged words), search engine marketing (SEM), or hot links. These have little or nothing to do with social media. SEO is a way of improving how many people can see your web site (visibility) through free or unpaid searches. These are sometimes called organic searches, for which you have developed mathematical formulas to determine which keywords to insert into your web site to increase its relevance to specific keywords that people are searching for. If, for example, you find that many people are searching for *free delivery,* you would want this term to be highlighted on your site so that your site will appear during Web searches. Because you are not paying a fee to have your site highlighted in the return back to the consumer, it can be buried in a multitude of other sites. With SEM, you pay a fee so that your site will appear either on the top of the search response (higher cost) or on the right-hand side of the page (lower cost).

I suggest companies that want to go down the social media path begin with simple and clear goals. Trying to sell a new product on a social page could end up failing miserably, while adding a moderator (someone to run the program and reply back to questions being posted) can add a significant number of interactions. Begin by searching for keywords being used within the largest social media sites, such as Twitter and Facebook. If you have an apparel line and want to find out how people feel about the latest fashions, just look for key terms that fit within your industry, like *soft fabric, bright colors,* and *matching pieces.* These terms will begin to give you a good idea of what consumers are looking for in a particular item. There are many tools that allow you to search for key terms in social blogging, including Google search. There are many very good tools and consulting firms ready to help you with your social media setup, including SAS, which I have seen in action and was impressed with.

Most social media efforts are geared toward a few simple goals: Build a group of consumers that you can follow (typically called a community), as these people will have their own followings. Track traffic that participates with your community or continues to use the phrases that you are interested in learning about.

As you do more searches, you will find that your brand or search term is showing up often with combinations of other words. Using these new words in combination with your original search can increase your hit rate (the chance of success in finding your brand). You need to continually update your lexicon, the library of words and phrases that grows as you find more terms that include your search criteria. If you find many blog entries that include your search term (your brand name) and the term *trendy,* you may want to add *trendy* to your search criteria and library of terms. This is called growing your lexicon.

There are certain individuals called influencers. These people are the ones that frequently forward out messages to their followers or friends and are sometimes called hubs of activity. If you can identify through your analytics team which people are behaving as hubs, you have a great opportunity to accelerate your product or brand awareness. Finding out what triggers an interest from this group is very important, and having a moderator stay in contact with these individuals is a good idea.

Your moderator will need a base of operations, or what is more commonly called a *community.* This can be as simple as creating a Twitter or Facebook page; even a page on LinkedIn is a great idea. These pages allow you to begin building a presence online that allows you to contact people or groups outside of your social media tracking. This also allows you to track the number of people who follow you or your brand. But there are some cautions:

- You must keep this page active with interactivity. You cannot let it get stale or appear abandoned; if you do you will quickly lose credibility.

- Do not get into sales mode. The social media community loses patience with people trying to solicit constantly from their page. If you have a product or service and you find someone asking for help, then you have an invitation to follow up. But to do so on a mass scale will quickly have people dropping you, as that is just not approved.

- Make your conversation current, and avoid shortcut texting unless you are extremely up to date on the current lingo. Abbreviations can get you into trouble if you're not sure what their meaning is. Be professional.

Remember to measure the things you can: the number of people who have responded with a mention of your brand (traffic), the number of times you have been included in a conversation, and the number of times your brand has been forwarded on to a group or community (influencer). These are all facts that can be tracked and measured over time. There are more, and with the right tools, you can set goals that will help you focus on the right media effort.

Glossary

Anchor Stores

In a mall, there are typically big-name retailers on each end of the building that are used to attract consumers. These big-name retailers are called *anchor stores*. Anchor stores are critical for the survival of most malls, as these are where the majority of consumers enter the building. Even open-air (no roof) malls have anchors at each end of the premises.

Artificial Intelligence (AI)

There are many different explanations of AI, so I will try to keep mine simple.

Humans tend to use the same reasoning when making decisions; they make these over and over again. The decisions are based on a learned experience, through which the results are seen over time. An AI tool is designed to put this behavior into a set of programs that can replicate this "learned" decision process millions of times, automatically.

Now when this process is replicated millions of times, patterns can become apparent (for example, results such as more sales and increased volume). Humans can learn from seeing the results and apply this knowledge to future decisions. What AI developers do is to apply these lessons into a system code that the computer can include in the decision process (that is, a decision tree). This implied learning is what artificial intelligence is all about. As positive or negative results are produced, the computer can use this information to improve the next set of decisions.

Back Stock

Back stock refers to merchandise that is still in the storage or stockroom.

Back Traffic Communications

Stores receive communications from headquarters as well as from other stores. This communication protocol is called *back traffic,* and can be scheduled to go to all stores or individual stores. These messages typically contain new promotion reminders, new merchandise advisories, and new labor hour reductions.

Basic Stock

These are products that are carried by the retailer all year long, with very little impact from seasonality on the volume sold. Basic stock products are typically placed in a standard display area with very little variability. In contrast, seasonal merchandise (such as Christmas candy) is displayed in an area that can be changed according to the season or holiday (called a *flex area*).

Catalogue, Circular, Roto, and Weekly Ad

These are terms used to describe promotional material that is sent to the consumer through direct market means. Walmart sends out one circular each month, while Kmart will send out a circular called the *roto* to millions of households each week. The number of pages can vary from as few as 10 to as many as 50, and is heavily dependent on the season.

C-Channel/Convenience stores

C-channel refers to smaller convenience stores, like the ones you find attached to gas stations. The stores typically contain a few staples and assorted small candy, chips, and soft drinks. They typically have a very large assortment of cigarettes and other tobacco products. The prices are usually slightly higher than the standard retail store, but you are paying for the convenience of buying merchandise as you fill up your car.

Centroid

A *centroid* is the center point within a polygon (that is, zip code, county, postal code). The centroid would be the center-most point within the area.

Customer Relationship Management (CRM)

The term *customer relationship management* is widely used in the direct mail business. The basic premise behind this term is defining who is managing the customer relationship. The term is being thrown about a lot lately, but it is extremely difficult to have a true CRM capability. There are now software and hardware tools that claim to immediately get you on the road to CRM, but remember, there are no real shortcuts in this field. From the information development side of the business, CRM means developing a centralized database that contains all of the consumer touchpoint data in one place. From this one location, you can effectively manage all the communication channels that reach the consumer.

Facings or Fronting

Each shelf in a store will have products on it. These products, as an example, might be bags of coffee. When there are five bags of the same product across the front of the shelf, this is called a facing. When an employee is asked to "face the counters," they are in fact being asked to bring all the products on a shelf to the front of the shelf (that is, full facing). The impression to the consumers as they walk down the aisle is that the shelf is well stocked and full. This also helps consumers to easily reach the product without having to reach deep into the shelf.

Floor Graphics

Many retailers today want to advertise inside the store as much as possible. To accomplish this, many vendors and manufacturers have developed large adhesive floor displays called floor graphics. These ingenious displays are placed directly on the floor in front of the products they are promoting. After the event or time period for the promotion, these graphics are removed by simply lifting them off the floor. They are held in place by a nonpermanent adhesive, and can withstand the stresses of customers running shopping carts over them.

Free On Board (FOB)

FOB is a transportation term that indicates the price of goods including delivery. In the receiving dock, this term is loosely used to indicate the receiving bill. The invoice terms usually inform the receiver of how long he has until the bill is to be paid before surcharges are added. This is typically 30 to 45 days (the retailer has 30 days to pay for the merchandise after it has been received). In a mass or grocery environment, a retailer would hope to sell two or more case pack deliveries before the bill date comes. In that case, the retailer is paying for the goods off of the interest of previously sold merchandise and not off the principal.

Haute Couture

Typically exclusive custom-fitted fashions with emphasis on high fashion, produced in Paris, New York, London, and Milan.

House Brands

These are products that do not carry a branded name such as Kellogg, Tide, or other easily recognizable names. Many retailers and especially supermarket chains will carry products with their own name. The same manufacturer is used to produce the house-branded product, but no license fee is paid for the brand name to be printed on the product. This can significantly reduce the price of the product, and again the savings are often passed to the consumer.

Hypermart

Hypermarts are extremely large retail stores, which generally carry a full line of grocery products as well as general merchandise and apparel. These stores tend to have other retail specialty shops like barbers, banks, shoe repair, nail salons, hair dressers, and photo studios, to name a few. They tend to be about 250,000 square feet (23,225 square meters).

Just in Time (JIT)

Just-in-time replenishment refers to receiving the merchandise you ordered just in time so that you do not run out of any merchandise. JIT shipment scheduling when done right can reduce the amount of money you have invested in merchandise that is sitting on the counter. This process can be extremely difficult to develop correctly, and typically requires partnering with a business that specializes in the logistics behind this process.

Key Performance Indicator (KPI)

When designing a test or analytics exercise, there are many different things you can test. Each test has a single most important business objective. To test for this objective, you need to define what it is you are testing for, and set the KPIs so that you know what to measure.

In retail, KPIs can include transaction counts, traffic counts, sales, gross margins, and so on.

Leaf Design

The leaf design is a store design in which each aisle in the store is set at a 45-degree angle to the main aisle. As you walk down the main aisle, you can see down multiple aisles at the same time. This is a more common design in Brazil and the rest of South America. The arrangement of the aisles resembles the veins of a leaf.

Lease Space

Many larger retail stores (supercenters) will have a section along the front of the store that gets leased out to local chains. These typically include bank branches, hair and nail salons, even optical offices. These spaces are leased from the store and can generate consistent revenue, while creating a nice destination draw.

Market Basket Analytics

Market basket analytics is a method for determining the differences between many different baskets of goods. As each basket can contain a different assortment of merchandise, basket analytics looks to find patterns or similarities between them.

Market Share/Fair Share

This is more of a philosophical point of view. When two competing retailers are in the same geographic location, they measure their market share based on the percent of expendable income they receive versus the competitor.

Your fair share could be the percentage of expendable income that is shared with competitors.

Consumers' expendable income is shrinking and their reliance on credit is growing. Is this a good thing? If most of the market that can get credit has credit, how do we grow?

Can you tell from your accounts how much spend is occurring on competitor cards? Yes, you can—sort of. Once you develop a pattern model of spend, any relative change to this pattern could be a purchase on another tender.

Another area that is of equal importance is the percent of expendable income (money left over after all the bills are paid). Lower income can translate to lower expendable income, which means less money to spend on food and entertainment (as an example). Where credit comes into play is the amount of cash resources people are willing to lay out versus the amount of credit, with which the payment comes later. Most households are unwilling to change a lifestyle choice when cash is limited, and as a result will enhance their lifestyle by using a credit vehicle.

Merchandise Hierarchy

Merchandise can be broken down into a hierarchy in which the highest level would be a division. From there it can be further segmented into department, category, subcategory, item number (SKU), and UPC. A single item number can have multiple UPCs assigned to it. A single paper plate can be sourced from multiple vendors. Each vendor will have its own unique UPC combination, which will roll into a single item number. Kmart had multiple suppliers for its 9-inch paper plates, including one for the East Coast and one for the West Coast. Each supplier had its own (supplier code) UPC, but the UPCs rolled up into a single SKU number. This was done for ease of replenishment and sales forecasting. Each retail organization has its own version of a hierarchy, some with more levels and others with less. But the underlying theme is being aware of the different classifications of the different products. This knowledge will not be lost on the retailer; it will even be appreciated.

Multitier Racks

These are typically 12-inch-long chrome hangers that stick out from the wall at different lengths. The purpose is to have multiple hangers that the clothes can be displayed on at varying distances from the wall, which creates a waterfall effect.

Next Best Offer (NBO)

Next best offer refers to providing a consumer that has recently purchased something from you an additional item that relates to the first product purchased. These types of offers are more common in the finance business—as you sign up for one product (for example, a checking account) the bank sends you an offer for another (perhaps retirement accounts). The science behind NBO is very complicated; to do it well requires at minimum a lot of research and data mining. You really need to understand how this consumer and his purchase relate to the thousands of others who have behaved in a similar fashion. You are identifying what the next logical purchase would be if the consumer had the ability to make it. Then you must make the offer before the consumer makes this purchase with a different business.

Overlapping Trade Area

Each store has a trade area, that area around a store where 70 percent of your customers come from. The overlap occurs when a zip code is included within multiple trade areas. Many retail chains will intentionally develop two different stores that overlap in trade areas to effectively lock out competitors.

Point of Purchase (POP)

Many manufacturers and vendors will supply special display units for their merchandise. These are typically freestanding and are placed on the sales floor. These are called point-of-purchase displays.

Polygons

Simply put, polygons are irregular shapes (for example, uneven rectangles). Examples would be a postal code that would encompass residential blocks, which are typically not square. Attributes such as sales penetration, where multiple variables are used, employ shading to distinguish different areas. Maps that highlight regions (polygons) are used by employing different colors or patterns.

Price Elasticity: Demand Curve

Typically, as the price of a good is decreased, the demand goes up (more is purchased), which is indicative of elasticity. Inelastic demand is commonly associated with necessities (for example, fuel or antibiotics), those products that are necessary and cannot be easily substituted. Conversely, soda (for example, Coke, Pepsi) is easily substituted. If the price goes up on one brand, the other will be purchased. There are many very complex studies and theories to support price elasticity demand curves, but I will not go that deep into them here. Caffeine is an inelastic product because of its lack of substitutes.

Product Turnover: Package Quantity Turnover Profit

Gross profit return on package quantity turnover looks at the number of items that are included in the shipping package. When the retailer orders stock to be delivered, most vendors will ship only in bulk (case packs), usually 6, 12, or 24 units. When the accounting department calculates margins, it frequently uses the total case pack to forecast revenue (margin management). If the frequency of the products being sold (turnover rate) is not fast enough, the retailer will have to pay for the products from profit. Ideally, three-pack quantities need to be sold before the FOB bill comes in. With this turnover rate, the retailer is paying for the merchandise from previous sales (interest on sales), not from margin.

Quadrant

As you look at a map of intersecting roads, they create four squares. In real estate, these are called quadrants. The northeast quadrant would be the top right quadrant. As we speak with field real estate representatives, they would tell us that there is an available site on the northeast quadrant of crossroads X and Y.

Radii or Radius

A radius map is a simple circle drawn around a center (centroid) point. Maps that contain multiple circles are called radii maps, and show one circle for each distance from the center (for example, one, three, and five miles).

Radio Frequency Identification (RFID)

Small devices are used to transmit signals through an electromagnetic spectrum on a special frequency. The RFID device contains an antenna that sends out a signal, and a second device has an antenna that picks up the signal and can read the information being sent. Some devices send out a price amount while others are used for security and tracking purposes.

Remote Maintenance Unit (RMU)

Remote maintenance units are carried around both large and small retailers today to enable area merchandisers to place orders for merchandise electronically. These small handheld devices are used to transmit signals through an in-store communications channel back to the main store office, which accepts the order. The associate scans a UPC bar code on the front of a shelf where the item sits. If the item is nearly out of stock, the associate places the order by scanning the bar code and entering the quantity to be ordered.

Retail Line of Trade

Each retail organization can have a different line, or trade, of merchandise, from heavy-duty equipment to consumables. Some even have groceries, apparel, and electronics all within the same walls. These types of retailers are often called hypermarts, or supercenters. These supercenters are typical in the 180,000 square-foot range or larger. For the hardcore retailer, hypermarts are actually even bigger supercenters and are over the 200,000-square-foot range.

There are category killers that specialize in just one type of merchandise. One example of this type of retailer is PetSmart. PetSmart carries only pet goods, but they carry a tremendous depth (wide assortment) of merchandise, far more than a typical mass merchandise retailer can carry. The prices are typically higher, but the one-stop shop and convenience is a big draw. These types of retailers are popping up everywhere these days because of their popularity and the availability of real estate. They need far less space than traditional retail stores, and can open in neighborhoods, making them far more convenient. A typical square footage would be around 60,000 to 70,000.

Runway

Every store has a runway, although they can be located in different locations. As you enter a store, the doors tend to lead you down a major aisle that takes you to the back of the store. These aisles tend to be larger, and can include bulk stacks of merchandise in the middle. Another form of the runway is located just in front of the POS registers. This aisle tends to be roomier in case the registers become backed up.

Season Codes

Merchandise is broken up into classifications across the country. Using the United States as an example, these geographies are typically set by weather climate zones (Northern, Southern, Eastern, Western, and Deep South). Products that are not influenced by seasons are often called basic merchandise (for example, detergents, books, and so on) and are carried across all stores, while apparel is heavily influenced by the climate. Stores (retailer locations) are also often organized into regions or divisions that are predicated on the seasonal zone that they fall into. This organization helps in a number of ways. One primary reason is to maintain a familiar merchandise look and feel for the consumer. Another big advantage is to keep the shipment of goods from the distribution center optimized. Logistics planning is a very big concern among retailers, and using seasonality can help in this area.

Season codes can also be tied back to a holiday season (for example, Christmas, Halloween, Easter, and Valentine's Day are some of the most frequent) when a specific group of merchandise is ordered for that holiday. As the date comes closer, you will usually find discounts on this merchandise. In the mass merchandise group, October through December sales can make up over 50 percent of a company's profit base.

SIC Codes

The term SIC is commonly used in business research. Standard Industrial Classification (SIC) codes are four-digit numerical codes assigned by the U.S. government to business establishments to identify the primary business (purpose) of the establishment. SIC is simply a numbering system that groups together similar products (services and businesses). The classification was developed to aid in the collection, presentation, and analysis of data and to promote uniformity and comparability in the presentation of statistical data collected by various agencies of the federal government, state agencies, and private organizations.

SKU Rationalization

Many retail companies today have over 60,000 individual SKUs (merchandise items). Larger retailers can have over 110,000 different items. As you bring on more new merchandise, the buyers are supposed to eliminate some lower-performing items to make room for it. SKU rationalization is the process of systematically removing SKUs from the total mix. Though there are many parts to this process, two of the more important steps are to make sure there are substitute products available for the consumer and to make sure you are not removing the items most important to your best customers.

Spatial Data Sets

Spatial data refers to addresses that have been converted to numeric coordinates (codes) called latitude and longitude points. These points can be found on maps. Spatial data sets are used to compare different geographic locations (for example, states, counties, zip codes). An example would be comparing the population bases of two different states and measuring the distance that divides them.

Sphere of Influence
This refers to the geographic area around a store location that would be considered the trade area.

Spinner Rack
Spinner racks are round displays that clothing items are hung on. These devices can be turned around so that you can stand still, while the articles of clothing turn.

Standalone, Strip Mall, or Primary Mall
A standalone store is typically bigger than a store built within a mall and can justify a parking lot dedicated to its customers. For the most part, these stores own their property, rather than leasing. The owner has to cover all of the maintenance costs. These establishments have multiple entrances.

Strip malls are popping up frequently, and in most cases near subdivisions and neighborhoods. As the name suggests, these stores are built in a line and typically follow the entrance toward the back. They have single entrances and are relatively small.

Primary malls are large groupings of a wide variety of stores. These have multiple entrances and can be multiple levels.

Stock-Keeping Unit (SKU)
A SKU is a retailer-assigned item number. Each retailer typically has its own version or form that is followed. There is no industry standard or formal protocol.

A typical general merchandise (GM) SKU might look like this:

DDDCCBBBBCS: 11 Bytes

Where

       DDD = Department Number
        CC = Category Number
     BBBB = Base Number
   and CS = Color Size Number

General merchandise usually comprises consumables, commodities, and household products.

A typical apparel SKU is 17 to 19 bytes, taking into account more seasons, styles, sizes, and shades of color.

Store Designs

Traditional stores: Typically carry just general merchandise and apparel (GM&A).

C-Channel stores: These are convenience stores attached to gas stations. They are very limited in their selection.

Store Intercepts: Exit Surveys and Focus Groups

Intercepts are a method of taking consumer surveys. One form is to stand outside of a store and ask every consumer a series of questions. Another form is to stand outside the competitor's store and ask the same set of questions.

Another way of gathering consumer information is to conduct focus groups. There will be a moderator who maintains the discussion and asks preselected questions. Most focus groups are "blind," which means the target company is not known. Many forums will provide a gift or other incentive to participate. The number of participants is limited to no more than 10.

Thematic Layers Data Sets

Thematic maps serve three primary purposes. First, they provide specific information (for example, population, income, age) about particular locations such as states, counties, and zip codes. Second, they provide general information about spatial patterns (for example, boundary outlines, shapes, and sizes). Third, they can be used to compare patterns on two or more maps. Thematic maps are sometimes referred to as *univariate,* or only displaying a single attribute or layer at a time.

Time Value of Money/Time Value of Time

The time value of money is usually associated with the interest earned over time on a base set of savings. Another way to look at it is that $1 today will be worth $0.90 in the near future because of the increased cost of living. But the time value of time refers to the inability to bank time. Time is a natural resource that is becoming scarce, and consumers would rather pay more for products to save time in shopping.

Topographical Layered Dissections

Topographical maps display different ground conditions and elevations, with dissections displaying different altitudes, such as depicting mountain ranges. Another example would be a map that displays shadings to differentiate various heights and ground conditions. The ground will be represented in shades of green for soil and grays for rock or mountainous areas.

Transaction Tagging

The process of adding identifiable consumer information to a transaction is called *tagging*. Many retailers would like to tag the largest percentage of transactions possible, without incurring the high cost of building a loyalty program. Many retailers collect zip codes as a proxy for addresses.

Transfer Sales

When you open a store within an existing store's trade area, you will lose some of the existing store's sales. This effect is called *transfer sales* because you are losing sales that transfer from an existing store to a new store. Typically, the sum of both stores' sales is large enough to keep both stores profitable while locking out the competition.

Univariate and Nominal Variables

In statistics, univariate refers to having only one random or independent variable. Nominal states refer to multiple variables being used.

Universal Product Code (UPC) Bar Code

UPC is governed by the Uniform Code Council, which sets the length and usage of the various forms of UPCs. This council has governing rights globally, and sets the parameters for all manufacturers and retailers. Each manufacturer is given a range of numbers that they are allowed to use. The most widely used type is the Standard 12 in the United States, while both EAN 8 and EAN 13 are frequently used in Europe. That being said, the Standard 12 is heavily used throughout the world now.

Big-box retailers, such as Kmart and Walmart, are given a retailer-assigned range of UPCs for internal usage. These retailer-use UPCs usually start with a 4 as the first digit.

A typical UPC would be 12 bytes, in the format: x-xxxxx-xxxxx-x. The first byte gives you the type of UPC (EAN8, and so on). The next five bytes are manufacturer identifiers, the next five are product identifiers, and the last digit is the check digit.

The UCC set a timeline for all manufacturers and retailers to be compliant with the standard by year-end 2005. This timeline was called "sunrise compliant." There are some additional types of bar codes, which, while not UPC, are making their mark and are showing up more frequently. The most prevalent of these are called Aztec bar codes and are set up as symbols that are typically square in shape, versus the traditional long bar code. The readers for these codes are much more expensive but the big win is that much more information about a product can be stored in this type of compressed coding.

White Lake Store Test

White Lake was a test bed for Kmart's new store design concept. We reduced the number of SKUs that we carried, but increased the amount of each SKU's merchandise in stock. This process helped reduce out-of-stock conditions while improving overall sales.

About the Author

Emmett Cox began his 27-year Kmart career gaining retail perspective by pushing shopping carts and stocking shelves in a Michigan store. Accepting increasing levels of responsibility, he continued to sharpen his store-level skills, advancing to operations manager. Promoted to Kmart headquarters in 1985, Emmett accepted roles of greater responsibility, including home electronics buyer, operations research project manager, strategic marketing leader, manager for real estate market strategy management information systems, and finally director of database marketing and information systems.

Emmett has been instrumental in the advances in market basket analytics and database design. He was the key subject-matter expert on using market basket data for strategic initiatives that included store location planning, merchandise mix modeling, logistics planning, price optimization, in-store department adjacencies, geodemographics analog modeling, assortment planning, and labor forecasting. In his last role at Kmart, he was directly responsible for managing outside agencies in the production of corporate and vendor-based targeted mail as well as the analysis of response measurement.

Emmett began his career with General Electric Money (GE Money) as the senior manager customer relationship management (CRM) analytics leader for the Walmart portfolio. He managed professional staff located in both the United States and India in the production of corporate and client-based analysis, built an understanding of the retailer's customers, leveraged internal and external data to define a portfolio strategy with clear financial goals, and managed client expectations for all analysis, data reporting, modeling, and strategic data requirements.

As GE's CRM leader in Australia and New Zealand, Emmett was instrumental in instilling a consumer-centric approach to analytics and creating the first full-time CRM position in the organization. Emmett worked in an executive consultative manner with Australia's leading merchants such as Coles (including Kmart and Target), Myer, Harvey Norman, and The Good Guys. The projects ranged in scope from real-estate site location, competitive response, and merchandise ranging to loyalty management and segmentation.

Emmett's most recent position within GE was global retail analytics leader, in which he led the retail loyalty management, credit card, and Internet strategies. Emmett's consultative approach was a success with both the GE portfolio businesses and the retail organizations directly. The projects included telecom loyalty in Russia, retail loyalty in the United Kingdom, retail analytics and loyalty management in Dubai (United Arab Emirates), Internet analytics in France, and retail loyalty in the Czech Republic.

Emmett has worked on a purely consultative basis with companies such as Precima, BBG-Global, and leading retail organizations. He was most recently leading the consumer insights and analytics within the Walmart financial services division.

Emmett is currently the senior vice president, consumer experience at BBVA Compass bank.

He continues to provide consulting expertise through many different channels around the world.

He has lectured in many CRM and marketing conferences and seminars, including the Paris Loyalty Forum, Czech Republic Loyalty Management, ACNielsen Category Management, Spectra Marketing and Intelligent Targeting, Teradata NCR Partners, and others in the United States; Coolum, Australia; and Vienna, Austria.

Index